America's 48th President and the Morning Star—the Two Kings of Tyre

Joel LivingGod

ISBN 979-8-89345-864-0 (paperback)
ISBN 979-8-89345-866-4 (digital)

Copyright © 2024 by Joel LivingGod

All rights reserved. No part of this publication may be reproduced, distributed, or transmitted in any form or by any means, including photocopying, recording, or other electronic or mechanical methods without the prior written permission of the publisher. For permission requests, solicit the publisher via the address below.

Christian Faith Publishing
832 Park Avenue
Meadville, PA 16335
www.christianfaithpublishing.com

Printed in the United States of America

To Americans and all who live under its influences.
Here's a personal letter to a family member of mine,
whom Christ used as a point of reference in attempts
to rescue this nation and all who dwell in it.
Not all who think themselves to be Christians truly
belong in the family of Christ. If you're reading this,
you too can be a part of Christ's true family.
If you're reading this, it's not too late.

Foreword

This book is basically a letter I was composing to enlighten my cousin named Solomon about life, spirituality, and my visions of woes to befall America, starting with the impending earthquakes signaled by the eclipse on April 8, 2024. The inception of the letter stemmed from his apprehensive perspective of the truth, which was based on lies permeated by the Western world. I soon realized that he, just like almost every one of my peers, had abandoned their foundational morals in favor of Western idiosyncrasies, which they've been slowly and unknowingly indoctrinated into. I wasn't an exception to such indoctrination prior to my spiritual awakening, which was sparked by the voice of God.

The letter to Solomon was intended to be a two-to-three-page message congruent to previous ones I had written to other family members. However, I couldn't stop writing this one, and by page 11, I realized that Solomon was being used as a reference for this generation, just like the character of Job in the Bible. Here we are, sixty-six pages and forty thousand words later. I had sleepless nights, neglecting my family for most of the eight days it took me to obsessively complete this message. As such, I must appreciate my wife, Ramera; my first son, Joel LivingGod Jr.; my second son, Obadiah LivingGod; and my lovely daughter, AraOluwa Urielle LivingGod, for sharing me with the world.

The true purpose behind this letter is to alert and awaken the world from its slumber as we must be prepared for the reign of America's forty-eighth president and Lucifer—the two kings of Tyre.

I'm not motivated by money but by a deep yearning to save souls, and I'll continually labor on behalf of people around the world until our Father in heaven calls me to glory.

Thanks to Yahuah Almighty, Christ our Savior, the Holy Spirit, my lovely mother, my wife and kids, my siblings, extended family, friends, fans, referenced authors, and all the true disseminators of Christ's unadulterated gospel. May the light of dispensation from Christ grant wisdom unto all readers and may the grace of our Father in heaven lead souls all over the world to true sources of His word and ultimately into righteousness. Hallelujah!

Preface

I've been compelled by the Holy Spirit to set aside all else to pen this message to you, for there's been a burning sensation in my heart that restrains me from doing anything else without fulfilling this task. This speaks to how our Father in Heaven earnestly yearns to draw you under His bosom, to endear you to His presence, and to have you witness His magnificence thereof. First, I'm thankful for the grace granted unto me from above, as I've been intimated to reckon with the importance of your transformation and impending testimonies. Secondly, I appreciate that you entrusted me with an opportunity to share the beautiful light of dispensation that has been granted unto me by the Holy Spirit to disseminate knowledge in accordance with the teachings of our Creator. This letter is intended to serve as a stern warning of things to come, how to possibly avert an impending judgment on America, and a pause button that allows you to transcend the simulation you're embedded in from an alternate perspective.

My message for you today is reflective of the fact that we live in a modern world that's at the furthest point away from our God Almighty, Yahuah. The vices and distractions we're embedded in have completely pulled our generation away from the recognizace of our entrenchment with all the things that misalign our purpose, thus derailing our understanding, with respect to who we are, who our God is, and what's expected of us. Most people of this era are like toads that were placed in a cool pot, devoid of understanding that the water has been turned up to the boiling point, spelling doom for them. Fret not, for I'm here to pull you out, and from the vantage point of salvation, you'll see the millions of boiling pots with your brothers and sisters unsuspectingly heated up to their demise, just as you and I were, and I promise you'll be compelled to play whatever part you can to wrestle their souls from the grasps of darkness.

Before proceeding any further, I want to alert you to events you're soon to witness in this world-dominating country, whose mighty wings cast a shadow over every other nation on this earth but isn't mighty enough to avert getting struck by lightning from the heavens.

Prophecy 1

The United States will witness a total eclipse on April 8, 2024, and although many are excited to see this event, what's unknown to them is that it presents a sign of judgment from God Almighty, whose true name is Yahuah. America has immersed herself in an array of full-scale evil perversions, schematic oppression, and all sorts of wickedness that condemn billions of innocent souls combined. This nation has been a proponent of effecting the will of the devil and has thus led unsuspecting souls all around the world to physical and spiritual condemnation. For this reason, God Almighty (Yahuah) is sending out a warning for the nation to repent. Just as Jonah was sent to warn the people of Nineveh of an impending judgment at the heels of an eclipse, I've been intimated to warn this nation. America has a total of seven places named Nineveh in the entire country, and the eclipse crosses every single one of them. There is also a Nineveh in Canada, and the eclipse crosses that as well. It is no coincidence that the United States is shaped like a whale, nor is it a coincidence that the eclipse occurs on the eighth and crosses over eight Ninevehs. The seven Ninevehs in the United States are in Virginia, Texas, Pennsylvania, Ohio, New York, Missouri, and Indiana. The lone Canadian Nineveh is in Nova Scotia.

Should America refuse to rend her heart in obedience to our Almighty Creator by April 8, 2024, or within forty days from then, lightning will flash across the gloomy afternoon skies. A trumpet will sound in the heavens, and it'll be perceived in the ears of man like thunder. The nation will experience a terrifying earthquake that'll split the land like a stiff loaf of bread. There'll be landslides, fire, chaos, and an air of unsettlement hovering over this mighty nation. Words cannot fully articulate the woe to come, but I plead for mercy on behalf of every soul. The people of Nineveh repented and were able to avert judgment, so I pray the same for America.

God's True Name

The name of the Christian God, Yahuah, was intentionally removed from the Holy Bible, and replaced thousands of times with "the Lord," "Lord," and "I Am That I Am." This was done by a conniving group of people who understood the power in His name and devised a grand scheme to keep it away from His chosen ones. Their plot has since been unraveled, and their senseless explanation hinges on two words, the "ineffable clause," meaning they removed the name Yahuah from the Holy Bible because it was too powerful to be mentioned. How so? Considering He expresses numerous times in the Holy Scriptures that He wants His people to know His name, and goes on to declare it plenty of times.

I just gave a prophecy, and for non-Christians, please note that only Yahuah has been documented to know the beginning of life from the end, and has proven such to be true by the fulfillment of prophecies given through His true prophets over time. The scriptures 'I will quote below will help prove this claim and simultaneously debunk the absurdity behind the complete removal of His true name from the Bible.

> "Present your case," says Yahuah. "Set forth your arguments," says Jacob's King. "Tell us, you idols, what is going to happen. Tell us what the former things were, so that we may consider them and know their final outcome. Or declare to us the things to come, tell us what the future holds, so we may know that you are gods. Do something, whether good or bad, so that we will be dismayed

and filled with fear. But you are less than nothing and your works are utterly worthless; whoever chooses you is detestable. (Isaiah 41:21–24)

That's Yahuah challenging lesser gods and idols worshiped by pagans. The purpose in that context was to show His supremacy over all other gods and establish His authorship of life and omniscience. The book of Isaiah, just like most books in the Bible, is filled with prophecies, all of which have come to pass in their entirety or are unfolding at the moment. King Cyrus of Persia was mentioned in Isaiah 44, written hundreds of years before he was born, and he did exactly what Yahuah declared. Here's an instance of Christ being able to do the same thing because He's one with God Almighty.

"You heard me say, 'I am going away and I am coming back to you.' If you loved me, you would be glad that I am going to the Father, for the Father is greater than I. I have told you now before it happens, so that when it does happen you will believe." (John 14:29)

Only God the Father, God the Son, and the true prophets who believe in them both can foretell the future with precision. Now I'll present scriptures with the alterations presented to the world by the purveyors of evil.

I am the Lord; that is my name! I will not yield my glory to another or my praise to idols. See, the former things have taken place, and new things I declare; before they spring into being I announce them to you. (Isaiah 42:8–9)

You see in the verse they claim the name of Yahuah to be "the Lord." I'll proceed to help you understand the effects of their slight.

AMERICA'S 48TH PRESIDENT AND THE MORNING
STAR—THE TWO KINGS OF TYRE

> Now Moses was tending the flock of Jethro his father-in-law, the priest of Midian, and he led the flock to the far side of the wilderness and came to Horeb, the mountain of God. There the angel of the Lord appeared to him in flames of fire from within a bush. When the Lord saw that he had gone over to look, God called to him from within the bush, "Moses! Moses!" Moses said to God, "Suppose I go to the Israelites and say to them, 'The God of your fathers has sent me to you,' and they ask me, 'What is his name?' Then what shall I tell them?" God said to Moses, "I am who I am. This is what you are to say to the Israelites: 'I am has sent me to you.'" God also said to Moses, "Say to the Israelites, 'The Lord, the God of your fathers—the God of Abraham, the God of Isaac and the God of Jacob—has sent me to you.' This is my name forever, the name you shall call me from generation to generation." (Exodus 3:1–2, 4, 13–15)

Please allow me to clarify the chaotic nonsense peddled by the alteration of God's true name in the referenced verses of Exodus. You clearly see how a variety of names were ascribed to the Christian God in a single encounter, and it was done with malicious intent. "I Am," "Angel of the Lord," "the Lord," and "God" are not names but titles, none of which Yahuah ascribed to Himself besides 'God. 'I received revelations about this through the Holy Spirit, so please allow me to explain what was hidden from the world in the verses I quoted above. The first reason behind the alteration is that which I previously expressed—to hide the true name of our Creator because His name holds the power to bind the demons of those who seized the scriptures from His true people and controlled the transcription of its contents to the entire world. The second reason was to hide the fact that it was two entities that appeared to Moses—God the Father, whose name is Yahuah, and God the Son, whose true name is

Yahusha (also known as Christ), who was described in verse 3 as the angel of the Lord.

Whenever you see "Angel of the Lord" in the Holy Bible, especially at the time of Moses, it refers to Christ our Savior. This means Christ (in spirit form) was the one who led Israel out of Egypt after He defeated all the lesser gods worshiped in Egypt by rendering them powerless. It was Christ who parted the seas and walked ahead of Israel in the pillar of fire and clouds. God Almighty, Yahuah, never left His throne to walk with man but always sent His Son Yahusha, who did everything commanded by His Father, first in spirit and then in flesh. There's confirmation of this assertion in many scriptures, so allow me to show you one in the scripture below.

> Yahusha replied, "If I glorify myself, my glory means nothing. My Father, whom you claim as your God, is the one who glorifies me. Though you do not know him, I know him. If I said I did not, I would be a liar like you, but I do know him and obey his word. Your father Abraham rejoiced at the thought of seeing my day; he saw it and was glad." "You are not yet fifty years old," they said to him, "and you have seen Abraham!" "Very truly I tell you," Yahusha answered, "before Abraham was born, I am!" (John 8:54–58)

Christ was making it known that He indeed appeared to Abraham, and had been with God's people from way before their time of captivity in Egypt. Readers of the scriptures wouldn't be able to identify such because His name was changed to the angel of the Lord. If His true name was left in the scriptures, any reader would've seen that Yahuah and Yahusha (God the Father and God the Son) appeared to Moses and sent Him to reveal the true name of Israel's God to the Israelites and the Egyptians. Allow me to show proof of Christ's encounter with Abraham.

> But the angel of the Lord called out to him from heaven, "Abraham! Abraham!" "Here I am," he replied. The angel of the Lord called to Abraham from heaven a second time and said, "I swear by myself, declares the Lord, that because you have done this and have not withheld your son, your only son, I will surely bless you and make your descendants as numerous as the stars in the sky. (Genesis 22:11, and 15–17)

Here you see Christ interacting with Abraham, but by the trickery of replacing His name Yahusha with "'Angel of the Lord'," they kept His divinity hidden, thus making it seem as though He was scripturally nonexistent before being born in the flesh. Christ was, is, and is to come, and although few Christians know of His existence from the beginning, none have been able to pinpoint His true deeds as I just conveyed to you. This is why Christ said in John 5:43, "I have come in my Father's name, and you do not accept me; but if someone else comes in his own name, you will accept him." Well, where do we see His Father's name in the Scriptures? And where do you see His name in the Scriptures? "'I am'" or "'the Lord'" doesn't bear any semblance or correlation to "'Jesus'," so please note that it was an intentional thing done to confuse the world based on much deeper reasons I'll explain later. For those wondering why the Pharisees lacked understanding of the underlying truth in the Scriptures, it's because they weren't true priests of Yahuah. Jews were under captivity at this time, and the high priests were handpicked by their oppressors, who were pagans and mostly sought to destabilize the religion of the true Jews.

These same oppressors oversaw translating the Scriptures from Hebrew to Greek, and they translated Christ's name from Yahusha to "'Ioesus'," which was later transliterated to English as "Jesus." They tricked the world into thinking Yahuah has many names when, indeed, He has one name and many titles. Christ also has one name (Yahusha) and many titles, including King of kings, the Lamb of God, the Messiah, the Lion of the tribe of Judah, and so forth. Like

Father like Son. Christians, be aware that there's power in the name of Jesus based on the faith we've attached to it over centuries, so this is not an attempt to devalue the foundation of faith you've built around the name. The truth is the truth, and I'm just a messenger 'here to help you understand that most of the truth you know is all lies. There's a lot of depth to why Christianity has been critiqued as contradictory, represented by innumerable denominations, or depicted as a false religion. Through this letter, I'll help debunk all these misconceptions by way of wisdom granted to me by the Holy Spirit.

Oftentimes you hear people say they're Christians, but their practice of faith is limited to just that claim. Being a Christian goes leaps and bounds beyond a statement or occasional prayers, but I'd be remiss if I blamed anyone for their lip-service Christianity, for I, too, was once a Christian by verbal affiliation. This brings us back to the point that our late modern era has been done a disservice by the rulers of men, people in high offices, and "'influential'" entities, whom the devil uses to suppress, subjugate, and coerce people into disobedience against our Creator, albeit for a little compensation, a taste of fame, or temporary power.

I once made a point that human understanding is grossly limited in capacity, citing the notion that one's mind only gets molded in accordance with what other people lead us to reckon with. For example, if you grow up in a cultural setting where it's customary for men to drink blood as a rite of passage, you, too, will drink blood. If your people worshiped idols carved out of wood, you too would worship those speechless dolls, for you wouldn't know any better. Things that seem abnormal to you are entrenched in the cultures and traditions of other peoples across the world, and it's a proven fact that human understanding is based on that which is taught to them, and what's seen around them.

The languages, morals, and principles of any human solely rely on what has been passed on to them by others. Simply put, our human understanding is very limited, and we easily become slaves to the things of the world, unless we're bestowed with God's wisdom. That's the inflection point the world is experiencing now, with

Western countries at the helm of doctrines and practices that corrupt the earth, enslaving all humans, young and old, rich and poor, free and slaves, into doing the will of the devil. Few have been given wisdom from above and are tasked with awakening the rest of the world from their slumber.

The Western world as you know it, is founded upon the worship of pagan gods, celestial beings, demons, fallen angels, and other evil entities. These conglomerates of otherworldly beings were once glorious angels and gods who were created by God Almighty (Yahuah) to do His bidding, or to nurture humans, the lesser entities He created. However, they acted in defiance and desired to exalt themselves instead. They were ultimately cast out of the heavens due to their disobedience, some onto the earth, while others remained bound to their duties until the day of judgment, when humans and all the otherworldly beings, including the sun and moon, will also be judged and condemned to their separate dungeons of eternal suffering.

There are levels to the evil entities I referenced, each with separate roles and influences on mankind. For example, demons are the legion of angels that got cast down unto earth with Lucifer after their rebellion led to a war in heaven, as seen in Revelation 12. Now they roam the face of the earth, inhabiting the minds of people who aren't fortified with the Holy Spirit, leading them to sinful acts like greed, addiction, theft, violence, sexual immorality, and so forth. They also afflict people with ailments of all sorts, and that's why every sickness Christ healed was categorized as an evil spirit being cast out.

Another example of rebellious entities is the "'sons of God'," also known as ""watchers," who were tasked to be the guardian angels watching over men. These watchers also rebelled against God Almighty and led men astray by teaching them the secrets of God's creation and how to make things from what's available to us here on earth (a.k.a. science). The watchers played some of the biggest roles in corrupting humans with information that should've been left unknown to man. They taught men to make weapons to kill each other, to wage war, and how to build pyramids to port celestial beings (sky gods) down to earth. They had humans thinking we could be gods of our own through science, and they even went further to have sex with our women, leading to the birth of the Nephilim (gigantic hybrid humans). I'll introduce scriptures to corroborate and lay emphasis on the message I'm trying to relay.

> When human beings began to increase in number on the earth and daughters were born to them, the sons of God saw that the daughters of humans were beautiful, and they married any of them they chose. Then the Lord said, "My Spirit will not contend with humans forever, for they are mortal; their days will be a hundred and twenty years." The Nephilim were on the earth in those days—and also afterward—when the sons of God went to the daughters of humans and had children by them. They were the heroes of old, men of renown. The Lord saw how great the wickedness of the human race had become on the earth, and that every inclination of the thoughts of the human heart was only evil all the time. (Genesis 6:1–5)

These Nephilim were mega giants that wreaked havoc on the earth, destroying God's precious creations including trees, animals, and even humans. The Nephilim built the great pyramids of Giza, of which the middle one was instrumental in porting sky gods from heaven unto earth. They presented a presence that corrupted the earth and all that dwelled in it, leaving God Almighty (Yahuah) no chance but to wipe them off the face of the earth in a flood. Yahuah gave several chances for mankind's repentance, but only Noah and his family were found to be righteous, thus being the ones who survived the judgment.

After Noah's flood, mankind would return to their defiant ways through the influences of the disembodied Nephilim, and through the legions of demons that were unaffected by the flood for they are spirits. The defiance of man once again culminated in them building the tower of Babel, under the supervision of a king and self-pro-

AMERICA'S 48TH PRESIDENT AND THE MORNING STAR—THE TWO KINGS OF TYRE

claimed god named Nimrod. Without spiritual insight, one would think the tower of Babel was merely a tall building that was intended to ascend quite literally into heaven. However, it was intended to be a giant ziggurat—a stepped pyramid that was used as a temple of worship to lesser gods, and to port celestial beings down from the heavens.

> Jacob left Beersheba and set out for Harran. When he reached a certain place, he stopped for the night because the sun had set. Taking one of the stones there, he put it under his head and lay down to sleep. He had a dream in which he saw a stairway resting on the earth, with its top reaching to heaven, and the angels of Yahuah were ascending and descending on it. He was afraid and said, "How awesome is this place! This is none other than the house of Yahuah; this is the gate of heaven." (Genesis 28:10–12, and 17)

That's an example to prove that certain locations are stargates, meaning they serve as a portal to the heavens. Yahuah opens the stargates for His angels to go back and forth from heavens unto earth, meanwhile, the demonic entities known as sky gods, teach man how to create these portals to port them down because they cannot do it for themselves. Having made this point, I'll bring your attention back to the Tower of Babel.

> Now the whole world had one language and a common speech. As people moved eastward, they found a plain in Shinar and settled there. They said to each other, "Come, let's make bricks and bake them thoroughly." They used brick instead of stone, and tar for mortar. Then they said, "Come, let us build ourselves a city, with a tower that reaches to the heavens, so that we may make a name for ourselves; otherwise we

will be scattered over the face of the whole earth." But Yahuah came down to see the city and the tower the people were building. Yahuah said, "If as one people speaking the same language they have begun to do this, then nothing they plan to do will be impossible for them. Come, let us go down and confuse their language so they will not understand each other." So Yahuah scattered them from there over all the earth, and they stopped building the city. That is why it was called Babel—because there Yahuah confused the language of the whole world. From there Yahuah scattered them over the face of the whole earth. (Genesis 11:1–8)

It's noteworthy that verse 7 of Genesis 11, uses an accompanying phrase, just like in Genesis 1:26, where Yahuah says, "Let us," meaning He wasn't alone during the first creation of mankind, and during the Tower of Babel decision, just as He wasn't alone during the call of Moses. I said "first creation" because after the creation in Genesis 1, Yahuah rested, and in Genesis 2 is when He specifically created Adam, who is the first ancestor of His chosen people. Anyways, Noah was the tenth generation from Adam, and Abraham was the tenth generation from Noah.

God made a covenant with Noah, symbolized by a rainbow, and a separate covenant with Abraham, referencing his descendants would be immeasurable like the stars in the sky. Noah survived the flood with his three sons namely Shem, Ham, and Japheth, and these were the people that would populate the entire world after the flood. Ham's grandson (Nimrod) was responsible for the Tower of Babel project, and he was the first human to be deified after his death, meaning he was assumed to have ascended to heaven, so his people worshipped him. The name Babel also means "gateway to heaven" in the language at the time, and a description of the tower can be found in a cuneiform tablet from Uruk. Nimrod worshipped the ancient Babylonian/Assyrian sky god named Marduk, who remains worshipped by many nations till date, including the United States of America.

One important point to reckon with is that Genesis 11 particularly states they intended to build a city, with a tower that reaches the heavens, meaning the tower would be erected within their nation. This bears semblance to what Egyptians did with the pyramids of Giza that was centered in their ancient city. The pyramids of Giza, just like the Tower of Babel, were both tasked to the Nephilim, and the proof lies before our very eyes that such a monumental feat is impossible to be accomplished by men. The pyramids of Giza consist of millions of precisely cut stones from a quarry hundreds of miles away from the site. No army of men, animals, machines, or entities today could accomplish such a feat, albeit with the "technological advancements" of the modern era. You'd be surprised how reliant the modern world is, on all the things taught onto man by the watchers, their seed (the Nephilim), and other sky gods. Now you can understand that evil spirits lead mankind to basic sin by defiling one's temple and hurting others, while celestial beings lead rulers of men to defy God on a much greater scale.

I've used my long-winded explanation as an opportunity to let you know that many nations are founded on the principles of evil, controlled by the principalities and powers influencing the rulers. Nations used to openly profess their worship of the lesser gods, as we've seen in ancient Egypt, Babylon, Assyria, Greece, and Rome, all of which had wicked rulers, remained at war, dominated the world, and filled their countries with monuments erected to the gods they worshipped. Such is the same with America, but unlike the ancient days when they openly professed their worship of lesser gods, these modern nations hide them in plain sight, and you'll only know the root of these things when the Holy Spirit calls your attention to it. You might be aware of the secret cults and societies like the Freemasons in America, and that the founding fathers of the US were Freemasons of the highest degree. Hence why you see pagan overtones like a pyramid, the eye of Horus, cult symbols, and other ancient Egyptian symbols on the US dollars.

The United States, its founding members, and current leaders mostly worship the gods of ancient Egypt. Osiris is one of the most popular gods of ancient Egypt, and he was cut into fourteen pieces by his jealous brother, Seth, who wanted to rule in his stead. Seth scattered the fourteen pieces of Osiris all over the Nile. Isis, the wife of Osiris, was able to recover thirteen of the pieces, and she later conceived a son for Osiris through magic. This son was named Horus, the hawk-headed god of ancient Egypt. I tell the tale of Osiris because the number '13' is significant to those who worship the ancient gods of Egypt, which is why you'll see it recurring in significance all over the Constitution of America.

Examples of the reverence given to the number 13 in America include the following: thirteen original colonies, thirteen signers of the Declaration of Independence, thirteen stripes on the US flag, thirteen steps on the pyramid, thirteen letters in "E Pluribus Unum," thirteen stars above the bald eagle, thirteen stars on the shield, thirteen leaves on the olive branch, thirteen fruits, and thirteen arrows. Also, it's almost impossible to find a thirteenth floor in America or a room numbered 13. Additionally, 'there are monuments raised to Egyptian gods all over America, including the 555-foot (× 12 = 6660) obelisk in Washington, positioned ahead of Ex-President Lincoln's memorial with his back to the temple, looking ahead at the obelisk facing east toward the sun.

> Then he brought me to the entrance of the north gate of the house of Yahuah, and I saw women sitting there, mourning the god Tammuz. He said to me, "Do you see this, son of man? You will see things that are even more detestable than this." He then brought me into the inner court of the house of Yahuah, and there at the entrance to the temple, between the portico and the altar, were about twenty-five men. With their backs toward the temple of Yahuah and their faces toward the east, they were bowing down to the sun in the east." (Ezekiel 8:14–16)

AMERICA'S 48TH PRESIDENT AND THE MORNING STAR—THE TWO KINGS OF TYRE

I share this scripture to reference two main points. First, being that Tammuz is yet another deified human that people worship till date. He was the son of Nimrod, who impregnated his own mother before his death. Yes, the same Nimrod responsible for building the Tower of Babel impregnated his mother before he was killed, and the offspring that came forth was Tammuz. Secondly, I'm using the scripture to point out how the sun god is worshipped, relative to what we see today. Men with their backs to the temple while facing east is a form of worship to the sun god known as Amun Ra to the ancient Egyptians, or Sol Invictus to the Romans. All nations, peoples, and cultures worship the sun in some form or capacity, ascribing several different names to it. Now that you know the identifiers for sun worship, one look at the Lincoln Memorial in Washington lets you know that America is not a nation founded on the Christian God as it's portrayed to be. You'll also see a pool of water reflecting the obelisk as if to say, "as above, so below." Inside the actual temple where Lincoln has his back turned, there's a painting of George Washington's ascension into the heavens, depicting that he's deified, just like Nimrod and Tammuz. Then go look at St. Peter's Basilica right in the heart of the Holy Roman Catholic Church (Vatican), which is supposedly a holy establishment. There you'll see statues of the ancient Greek and Roman gods lined up with their backs to the temple, looking ahead at the obelisk facing east, once again in honor of Amun Ra or Sol Invictus, the sun god.

The Roman Catholic Church First Beast of the End Times

The Roman Catholic Church is a demonic establishment that represents the first beast of the end times. They're described in the scriptures as the clay that holds together the nations that will wreak havoc upon the chosen ones of Yahuah in the final chapter of humanity as we know it. The Catholic Church put everyone in the cool pots under the guise of being representatives of Christ but has since used the nations under their supervision to slowly turn the heat up, literally killing millions of people over time, and subjecting the souls of many more unto destruction. The pagan 'holidays' celebrated all over the world were implemented and popularized by the Catholic Church, and they're nothing but feasts and festivals offered to their lesser gods. Simple research into the pagan origins of days we observe in the modern world would unveil what they truly represent, what was normally done in those days, and how they whitewashed it under the guise of Christianity. Christmas (Saturnalia), Valentine's Day (Lupercalia), Halloween (Samhain), and Easter (for goddess Ishtar) are all founded on paganism. Christ wasn't born on December 25 and the true beginning of the year is in Spring, not January. The day of Yahuah's worship is the Sabbath (Saturday), but they changed it to Sunday in honor of their sun god. The days of our week, the names of the months, and much of the English verbiage are interwoven with the names of pagan gods and derivatives of their demonic festivals.

For example, the "planets" are called Mercury, Venus, Jupiter, Pluto, Saturn, etc. These are all names of pagan gods in the Greek and Roman pantheon of deities. Also, these 'planets' are not planets, but celestial beings that are alive and influential in stirring man away from God almighty. The Roman Catholic Church uses the nations under its control (European countries) to disseminate a bunch of misinformation about life, to masses all over the world. When you attain some spiritual discernment, you'll understand why a supposedly holy establishment is basically a shrine filled with a bunch of pagan gods and monuments. I know it may seem difficult to give up some of these pagan holidays, but I must inform you that our true God, Yahuah absolutely loathes these days which are nothing, but feasts offered unto lesser gods.

> Nevertheless, I have this against you: You tolerate that woman Jezebel, who calls herself a prophet. By her teaching she misleads my servants into sexual immorality and the eating of food sacrificed to idols. (Revelation 2:20)

> "And now, you priests, this warning is for you. If you do not listen, and if you do not resolve to honor my name," says Yahuah Almighty, "I will send a curse on you, and I will curse your blessings. Yes, I have already cursed them, because you have not resolved to honor me. "Because of you I will rebuke your descendants; I will smear on your faces the dung from your festival sacrifices, and you will be carried off with it." (Malachi 2:1–3)

"Jezebel" in the first scripture is metaphorically used to represent the Roman Catholic Church. It's apparent from these scriptures that our Creator detests the holidays most people unknowingly celebrate in honor of pagan gods. Now that you know, it'd be pure ignorance to wallow in the pool of obscenities. Valentine's Day is mainly a day of lust and sexual immorality with the demons it honors making matches of incompatible souls, causing such unions to end in violence, trauma, heartbreak, single parents, and fatherless children. I understand 'there are married couples or soulmates in observance as well, but the bigger picture is that broken relationships make up the bigger picture of unions in our modern world. I wish there was a nicer way to convey this message, but I refuse to dumb down the truth of our God Almighty which I've been recruited to pass along in its entirety. I'm not a megachurch or a worldly preacher who says what people want to hear or follow along with evil doctrines to build a following. I seek nothing from this but to win souls for our Father in heaven. The Catholic Church is a political organization that uses Christ as a cover-up. That's why they refuse to observe the true feasts mentioned in the Holy Scriptures, but instead formed several holidays that have the world celebrating the feasts of their gods and other deified humans they call '*saints*.' WAKE UP!

Remember they taught you in school that humans evolved from monkeys? Remember they said the world came about by way of a big bang? What a big lie! The purpose of teaching such jargon is to take credit away from Yahuah, and to disenfranchise us from being aware that our Creator made this beautiful world for us to enjoy. They used Western education to give credit to humans (scientists) as opposed to Yahuah Almighty, the Omniscient being.

> Then God said, "Let the land produce vegetation: seed-bearing plants and trees on the land that bear fruit with seed in it, according to their various kinds." (Genesis 1:11)

> God made two great lights—the greater light to govern the day and the lesser light to govern the night. He also made the stars. God set them in the vault of the sky to give light on the earth, to govern the day and the night, and to separate light from darkness." (Genesis 1:16–18)

AMERICA'S 48TH PRESIDENT AND THE MORNING STAR—THE TWO KINGS OF TYRE

> Yahusha said, "There will be famines and earthquakes in various places. All these are the beginning of birth pains." (Matthew 24:7–8)

Creation is meticulously detailed and woven into a network of interdependence among all living beings, including the Earth itself, which most people don't credit for being alive but in fact is. Christ correlates earthquakes to the birthing pains of the Earth. Likewise, the sun and moon were given authority to "'govern','" showing 'there is life in these things. An array of complex, inexplicable events like volcanic eruptions and famines should intimate to you that this rock called Earth is indeed alive. The Earth gives birth to new lands through volcanic eruptions, whereby out of nothing comes a delivery of new islands, each teeming with their own network of plants, trees, and all sorts of new life. That's the Earth giving birth, and Christ even says in Matthew 3:9 that God can raise children from stones, meaning God can breathe life into that which you think is rendered lifeless. I mean, the waters did part to allow the Israelites safe passage through the Red Sea, and through the Jordan River, respectively. Proof has since been documented of these events for those who doubt the exactness of such miracles.

The Sun isn't a raging ball of fire as it is so described by "'scientists'" who know nothing, but a fringe of God's creation as revealed to them through their lesser gods. When Amun Ra was leading the nation of Egypt along with a host of other gods like Seth, Isis, and Osiris, the Egyptians had a Mystery School of Sciences where these sky gods taught them deep secrets of Yahuah's works. Such schools helped produce *The Book of Thoth* by Thoth Hermes Trismegistus, who was revered as a communicator with the gods. The topics covered in *The Book of Thoth* include art, music, law, alchemy, medicine, philosophy, mathematics, geography, anatomy, and chemistry.

Egypt's Mystery School of Sciences is where renowned philosophers, stonemasons, scientists, artists, and alchemists all learned ""Satan's so-called deep secrets"" mentioned by Christ in Revelation 2:24. Pythagoras learned the secret rules of numbers, astronomy, music, and mathematics, which helped him come up with things like "Pythagoras' theorem, taught in modern textbooks that were spread by European countries. The Egyptian priests (or Magi) of the Mystery School had other Greek students like Plato, Thales, and Orpheus. Hippocrates studied medicine there, along with other notable people who became known as the founding fathers of medicine. Greek philosophies were founded on all the knowledge gained from the Mystery Schools in Egypt, and the Romans, upon conquering the Greeks, incorporated everything the Greeks had learned into the Greco-Roman era of Classical Antiquity, serving as a foundation of everything we're taught today.

I mention these things because those were the founding fathers of Western education, medicine, theories, and philosophies. They learned everything from the Egyptian Mystery Schools and went on to form the textbooks and educational curriculums passed around the world. That's why all science textbooks completely exclude our Almighty Creator from everything by coining fictitious theories like the Big Bang, which I call The Big Lie. These scientists also claim mankind evolved from monkeys, and that all life came from non-life, meaning a clash of rocks banged and separated into different planets, including the sun, moon, stars, and so forth. After the Earth supposedly separated from the bang, it produced rocks and water, which eventually gained wisdom to create simple life on its own, incepted inside the waters and supported by a self-made cycle of light, weather, and seasons. From there came the "'subphylum Vertebrata'" that explains how classes of sea creatures like Agnatha (hagfish), Chondrichthyes (stingrays), and Osteichthyes (tuna) evolved into Class Amphibia (frogs and salamander), which evolved into Reptilia (snakes and tortoises), which later evolved into Class Aves, consisting of all birds like eagles, penguins, swans, and ostriches, which then evolved into Class Mammalia (monkeys, gorillas, and humans). I learned this in my junior year of college and was very fascinated, without knowing I was being fooled.

To surmise the bogus evolutionist theory: gas evolved into living things, turtles became elephants, and tadpoles became humans. That's the story sold by science to man, supported by spurious claims that these things happen over billions of years, because, of course,

AMERICA'S 48TH PRESIDENT AND THE MORNING STAR—THE TWO KINGS OF TYRE

no one would be alive to be a witness. There's no such thing as evolution, and only a dull mind will believe such fallacy after reading this letter in its entirety. Yahuah created everything you see, just as they were, and the only permissive exclusion in the genetic coding of species is a thing called adaptation—meaning all species can develop adaptive features encoded in their DNA for increased survivability of their species down the line. An example would be the increased lung capacities of humans living at higher altitudes, or sheep developing thicker fur based on the rigid temperatures they migrate to. It doesn't mean one rabbit will grow tired of being hunted and hold a meeting to turn all rabbits into lions, or that a toad that's tired of being stepped on will evolve into a giraffe.

These are all lies they sold to the masses, and I'll help you understand that our Creator is a fascinating artist with an artistic signature pattern that intricately translates across all species. His signature is called Metatron's Cube—it encompasses all geometric shapes in existence, and all patterns found in all lifeforms of every created being, including inanimate objects. Other intangible elements of Yahuah's signatures are revealed through mathematical formulas like the "Flower of Life," the "Fibonacci Sequence," and the "Mandelbrot Set," all of which show the patterns used to fashion every species of plants, animals, cells, insects, and inanimate objects like landscapes, shells, snow, and even lightning. Watch a YouTube video titled "Science Finds the Mind of God" (on the Video Advice Channel). The Mandelbrot Set goes further to reveal how infinite the works of Yahuah truly are, because if you zoom into a tiny fringe of the pattern, it continues into an infinite array of new patterns that are uniquely different and perpetual.

> The realm of the dead is naked before Yahuah; Destruction lies uncovered. He spreads out the northern skies over empty space; he suspends the earth over nothing. He wraps up the waters in his clouds, yet the clouds do not burst under their weight. He covers the face of the full moon, spreading his clouds over it. He marks out the

horizon on the face of the waters for a boundary between light and darkness. The pillars of the heavens quake, aghast at his rebuke. By his power he churned up the sea; by his wisdom he cut Rahab to pieces. By his breath the skies became fair; his hand pierced the gliding serpent. And these are but the outer fringe of his works; how faint the whisper we hear of him! Who then can understand the thunder of his power?" (Job 26:6–14)

The key lesson from that passage is that all the glory your naked human eyes see of Yahuah's wonders are but the outer fringe of His works, as articulated through the infiniteness of the Mandelbrot Set. Please note that mathematics, just like other sciences, was not invented by man, but unlike other studied subjects, mathematics isn't physically substantiated and only exists in the mind, as a governing rule to explain small fractions of God's creation. Mathematics, through the discovery of these expressed formulas, also gives a peek into the mind of Yahuah, by asserting the fact that an inexplicable, un-understandable, omniscient mind designed everything in existence. Yahuah is Science, Yahuah is Mathematics, Yahuah is Law, Yahuah is Spirit, Yahuah is Technology, and all the studied subjects combined. The lesser gods taught men to exclude Yahuah from everything and accredit it to themselves as geniuses, in exchange for reverent worship of their "sky gods" to whom they'd erect monuments.

There's an old Yoruba proverb that says, "in the land of the blind, the one-eyed man is king." Humans are the blind in this instance, and the one-eyed kings are the lesser gods who make men worship them based on their "divine abilities" and "higher knowledge," which is true, but only in comparison to man.

These otherworldly beings are denoted as "sky gods" or "Anunnaki" from another planet, but there's no such thing as another planet, since Yahuah only created the Heavens (plural) and one Earth, as seen in the first sentence of the Holy Bible: "In the beginning Yahuah created the heavens and the earth." There are a few heav-

AMERICA'S 48TH PRESIDENT AND THE MORNING STAR—THE TWO KINGS OF TYRE

ens, and they serve as an abode to a variety of celestial beings, with Yahuah being in the highest heaven. Celestial beings include what we know as stars, planets, constellation clusters, the sun, and the moon. Contrary to what science has led the world to believe, these entities aren't just balls of gases or lifeless rocks in the skies.

They're all alive and serving their purpose until this world as we know it comes to an end. How is a ball of fire (the sun) able to give life to plants and vitamins to humans? Why not create a bonfire or light a torch and have that give you vitamin D? Why is the moon linked to the physiology of humans and other animals, serving as a determining factor for their reproductive cycles, fertility, and menstruation? This is besides the fact that the moon also plays a pivotal role in our circadian rhythms—the mental, physical, and behavioral changes organisms experience over a twenty-four-hour cycle. Even the oceans are subject to the effects of the moon through its "gravitational pull," thus causing high tides and low tides, also within a twenty-four-hour cycle. These were duties Yahuah assigned to all these celestial beings, to nurture, govern, and keep the cyclic nature of life in synchrony and continuance, just by being what they are. Likewise, humans were created and granted the powers to nurture, govern, and control things on the Earth, and to multiply, just by being what we are.

> And God said, "Let there be a vault between the waters to separate water from water." So God made the vault and separated the water under the vault from the water above it. And it was so. God called the vault "sky." (Genesis 1:6–8)

The sky is a vault that's locked, and that's why these sky gods influence humans to build stargates to unlock them. Hence why you see a prevalence of stargates (Ziggaruts and pyramids) in ancient civilizations like those of the Assyrians, Egyptians, Babylonians, Persians, and Mayans.

If you wonder how these celestial beings can influence mankind into doing these things, please remember I already intimated you to the fact they were created with abilities to affect our physiology, including our minds. Hence why sometimes you get in the sun and feel alive, or you feel a magnetic energy by being under the light of the moon or are innately inspired by staring at the stars. These beings were given abilities to affect mankind to the very core, so now you can have a different perspective of why Yahuah said, "Let us," according to Genesis 1.

> And God said, "Let there be lights in the vault of the sky to separate the day from the night, and let them serve as signs to mark sacred times, and days and years, and let them be lights in the vault of the sky to give light on the earth." And it was so. God made two great lights—the greater light to govern the day and the lesser light to govern the night. He also made the stars. God set them in the vault of the sky to give light on the earth, to govern the day and the night, and to separate light from darkness. (Genesis 1:14–17)

> Then God said, "Let us make mankind in our image, in our likeness, so that they may rule over the fish in the sea and the birds in the sky, over the livestock and all the wild animals, and over all the creatures that move along the ground." (Genesis 1:26)

The simple minds of humans will overlook intricate messages in the biblical story of creation, but it's important to note that with Yahuah's wisdom, you can deduce in the story that celestial beings were created to rule mankind and that mankind was created to rule all the creatures on earth. There's a hierarchical arrangement by our Creator, but the celestial beings became corrupt, jealous, and desiring of worship for themselves, so they introduced themselves to man, presenting a supremacy that forced simple minds to worship them over our true Creator. We see the sky gods also influence mankind into such a mindset of supremacy where a race of humans sets themselves above another race, using the knowledge given to them by these gods to subdue those they consider to be the inferior race. All topics learned at the Egyptian Mystery School, including science, law, philosophies, weaponry, alchemy, and spirituality, are used by the race who consider themselves superior, over the race they think to be inferior.

Separate nations are ruled by separate gods, who lead the nations they govern into war against nations governed by other gods. These gods fight to dominate mankind and teach mankind to dominate each other as well. For example, Ancient Babylon was initially governed by the sky god Marduk, and Ancient Egypt was governed by Osiris, Isis, Seth, and so forth. The gods of Egypt fought for internal control, like Seth killing Osiris. Then they'd also lead their nation (Egypt) to wage war against the nation of Babylon controlled by their arch-nemesis Marduk. If your eyes were opened by Yahuah, you'd see the chariot of seven horses pulling the sun, who is a celestial being without legs.

If your mind was opened, you'd understand that ancient sun gods like Ashur were depicted as having no legs and are usually carved with replacement limbs of a lion or some skirt to hide the absence of his legs. In some religions, the moon is also worshipped, either individually or alongside the sun. For example, King Nebuchadnezzar II of Babylon worshipped many gods including Inanna, who is also known as Ishtar, a moon goddess. Ishtar is known as the goddess of love, war, and fertility, and her festival day was sold to us as Easter, which is a syncretism of her worship into Christianity by the evil Roman Catholic Church.

Now you see there's an agenda, and you know the main body behind such, so I'll pick up from the nations and "spiritual" establishments of this era, for they are founded on the worship of those same gods of ancient times. The three pyramids of Giza are aligned with a slight curve through their tips to match the belt of Orion in the heavens. So also, you have three obelisks in New York forming the same exact pattern to match the placement of Orion's Belt in the skies above. These things reveal nations that are founded upon the worship of celestial beings and are led by those entities to do wicked things to remain in power. Hence why the founding of America involves bloodshed and wickedness, and its continued dominance has relied on slavery, and the systematic annihilation of leaders in foreign countries. Millions of lives have been lost to local wars initiated by America, after which America would then go on a mission to 'restore peace' in such nations. In fact, they destabilize these nations and leave them worse off, own them, and own their resources by installing a ruler that reports to them. You'd be surprised how many countries are under the tightly tensioned lock of America's talons. The importance of pointing these things out is to pass along the message that's been given to me for America to repent from these sins or face the wrath of Yahuah.

Almost every religion claims to have a creator god who made everything, but none of them can sensibly articulate how they supposedly fashioned things into existence. Their creation stories are all based on what their specific god claims, but those claims are never substantiated by any credible sources except their one prophet, making claims of visions from a supernatural being. Christianity may be met with such accusations as well, but it's important to note that when comparing Christianity to other religions, there are significant differences on so many levels. The claim of Yahuah's supremacy does not come from one single prophet, but from dozens of prophets over thousands of years. Yahuah's supremacy isn't registered in the history of one nation but memorialized in the history and writings of all ancient kings and kingdoms like Assyria, Babylon, Egypt, Persia, Greece, and Rome. Christianity is the only religion that other religions are fighting to align themselves with or making comparisons to. Yahuah's temple in Jerusalem is the only holy site in the world that several nations and religions of other peoples have fought to claim. Greek, Roman, and Arabic gods have all influenced men to stake their claims on the temple or it's site over time, and they'll continue to do so until they erect the final temple that combines all these religions in a few years. You'll never see or hear of the Christian God influencing men to go conquer the site of any temple belonging

AMERICA'S 48TH PRESIDENT AND THE MORNING STAR—THE TWO KINGS OF TYRE

to other gods, just to build a temple for Yahuah on it, but you see it happening the other way around.

My concern isn't with all that right now and this letter is specifically to focus on America and the warning I've been tasked to pass along. This nation wickedly continues to shroud the truth regarding the true identity of the people of Yehuda, misaligning who black people truly are with a group of people that assumed their identity under false pretenses.

> To the angel of the church in Smyrna write: These are the words of him who is the First and the Last, who died and came to life again. I know your afflictions and your poverty—yet you are rich! I know about the slander of those who say they are Jews and are not, but are a synagogue of Satan. (Revelation 2:8–9)

> I will make those who are of the synagogue of Satan, who claim to be Jews though they are not, but are liars—I will make them come and fall down at your feet and acknowledge that I have loved you. Since you have kept my command to endure patiently, I will also keep you from the hour of trial that is going to come on the whole world to test the inhabitants of the earth. (Revelation 3:9–10)

These were the words of Christ in relation to the end times. Christ sends warnings to Smyrna and Philadelphia, both of which are in modern-day Turkey. Simply put, the supposed Jews everyone refers to as the chosen people of Yahuah are not the true Jews. They are the Khazars—a nomadic Turkic people that settled across southeast Europe including Russia, Ukraine, and Kazakhstan. The fact they impersonate Jews is part of fulfilling prophecy according to the scriptures. Israel was warned by Yahuah to refrain from worshipping idols like the other nations. The promise was that if Israel participated in idol worship, then other idol-worshipping nations would be raised to conquer them. These prophecies were fulfilled in the time of Babylon, Greeks, Romans, Islamic Caliphate, and the European slave trade. All these events fall under the section of the first beast of the end times (Roman Catholic Church) because they were instrumental in coordinating the foolery that scrambled the identity of the true Jews.

My calling is recent, so I couldn't warn Turkey in advance, but the first three chapters in The Book of Revelation open with specific messages to seven locations that are all in Turkey. For those unaware, much of the physical location known as Turkey used to be Greek settlements, so the judgment wasn't only reserved for the Turks but also for the Greeks who initially settled on that land, and the Romans who later conquered them, before it was finally conquered by the Ottoman Empire under the Islamic Caliphate of Mehmed V. There's a ton of significance behind the messages given by Christ to those locations in Turkey, especially the emphasis on "'Fake Jews'" in Revelation 2 and 3, respectively. Besides that, the referenced chapters call for repentance and warn of an impending judgment, some of which came into effect by way of devastating earthquakes on February 6, 2023. These earthquakes and subsequent aftershocks formed a figure "7' pattern along the location of the seven places mentioned by Christ. An approximation of 60,000 lives were lost with over 140,000 people injured.

Remember, *Christ said, "There will be famines and earthquakes in various places. All these are the beginning of birth pains" (Matthew 24:7–8).*

Prophecy 2

Yahuah's holy city will be built on new lands uninhabited by man. This means the earth will give birth to new lands for the millennial reign of Christ. The earthquakes are likened to birthing pains because the earth is getting ready to birth new lands as I previously intimated you to it being a living being. The chosen people have been scattered across the world over time and are being gathered, just so they can be led once again to a promised land. The earthquakes will come first, then volcanic eruptions triggered by things I might mention later.

Now I'll proceed to highlight the sins of Yahuah's chosen people, why they were scattered, where it was prophesied, how they're being gathered, their true identities, and what must be done for them to avoid being afflicted during the judgment of the wicked.

> Be careful not to forget the covenant of the Lord your God that he made with you; do not make for yourselves an idol in the form of anything the Lord your God has forbidden. For the Lord your God is a consuming fire, a jealous God. After you have had children and grandchildren and have lived in the land a long time—if you then become corrupt and make any kind of idol, doing evil in the eyes of the Lord your God and arousing his anger, I call the heavens and the earth as witnesses against you this day that you will quickly perish from the land that you are crossing the Jordan to possess. You will not live there long but will certainly be destroyed. The Lord will scatter

you among the peoples, and only a few of you will survive among the nations to which the Lord will drive you. There you will worship man-made gods of wood and stone, which cannot see or hear or eat or smell. But if from there you seek the Lord your God, you will find him if you seek him with all your heart and with all your soul. When you are in distress and all these things have happened to you, then in later days you will return to the Lord your God and obey him. For the Lord your God is a merciful God; he will not abandon or destroy you or forget the covenant with your ancestors, which he confirmed to them by oath. (Deuteronomy 4:23–31)

The quoted scriptures prophesy the dispersion of Israel and Jews into captivity, which is quite indicative of what happened to Africans during the transatlantic slave trade. Before I proceed, allow me to introduce an elusive fact that the Transatlantic Slave trade was ordered by the Roman Catholic Church, through Pope Nicholas V who issued a decree called the Dum Diversas Papal Bull of 1452, issued by Pope Nicholas V. This granted King Alfonso V of Portugal the rights to invade, destroy, and subject Africans (described as sub-human), to perpetual slavery, for the purpose of profit. I'll let you read an excerpt for yourself.

We weighing all and singular the premises with due meditation, and noting that since we had formerly by other letters of ours granted among other things free and ample faculty to the aforesaid King Alfonso—to invade, search out, capture, vanquish, and subdue all Saracens and pagans whatsoever, and other enemies of Christ wheresoever placed, and the kingdoms, dukedoms, principalities, dominions, possessions, and all movable and immovable goods whatsoever held and possessed by them and to reduce their persons to perpetual slavery, and to apply and appropriate to himself and his successors the kingdoms, dukedoms, counties, principalities, dominions, possessions, and goods, and to convert them to his and their use and profit—by having secured the said faculty, the said King Alfonso, or, by his authority, the aforesaid infante, justly and lawfully has acquired and possessed, and doth possess, these islands, lands, harbors, and seas, and they do of right belong and pertain to the said King Alfonso and his successors." (Pope Nicholas V on behalf of The Roman Catholic Church)

The pope would later make additional decrees that included how other European countries could join the frenzy of enslaving Africans. In essence, the Popes of the Roman Catholic Church authorized European countries to kill, rape, own, steal, and destroy the lands and possessions of Africans, all in the name of Christ. It's quite jolting, and I wept on the day I was led in spirit to this discovery. Now you can identify that certain people use Christianity solely for political reasons. When you see such things, be careful not to criticize Christianity because the devil has influenced so many malicious things against the religion of Christianity in attempts to discredit it.

Not all who claim to be Christians are true followers of Christ. A lot of people and institutions are masquerades who pretend to be aligned with Christ but are indeed agents of Satan. This is why Christianity has endured much criticism and claims of contradictory practices. The true Church described in the Holy Scriptures is totally different from what these establishments and governments push in the modern era, including how most megachurches have become grounds for political rallies or spokespersons for normalizing condemned behaviors. Church was intended to be a true fellowship of people, but greedy humans with ulterior motives have turned the religion into a political weapon, and a fiasco of denominations that mostly antagonize each other. Please don't allow these agents of the devil to lead you straight to hell by affiliation. Pray in your heart for guidance. Yahusha will speak to you directly or lead you to worship through trusted agents of His truth. You can pray in your home and fellowship with your family, and eventually, you'll be led through the Holy Spirit to find a community of true Christians.

Abraham's descendants were promised to cover the earth like dust. Only one race of people fulfills that prophecy. Israel was prophesied to be scattered across nations into captivity. Only one race of people fulfills that prophecy, as black people have historically been the enslaved race throughout history. Black people are the ones who have suffered the captivities prophesied in the Holy Bible. Black people are still the ones systematically oppressed and hated all over the world, including America, just for being black.

When the Europeans invaded Africa equipped with their ancient maps of the 1700s, a specific portion of Africa on those maps was marked as Negroland. This Negroland on their map is known today as West Africa. They also marked the portion by the Niger River as "Kingdom of Juda," meaning they know who those black people were, and they went for them specifically. Remember these nations are guided by the lesser gods they serve, and these gods know Yahuah's people, thus targeting them. The initial slavers were the Western Ashkenazi Mongols who infiltrated Portugal and Britain. These slavers enlisted the help of Islamic trappers to infiltrate the kingdom of Judah. Once again you can revert to the current location known as Turkey and notice how the three primary groups of people that emanate from there (Greeks, Romans, and Islamic Caliphate Arabs) are historic oppressors of Yahuah's chosen people.

That's why verses 30–31 of Deuteronomy chapter 4 are critical for black people to know what's required of them from Yahuah, their true God, not the lesser gods worshipped by these nations.

> O God, do not remain silent; do not turn a deaf ear, do not stand aloof, O God. See how your enemies growl, how your foes rear their heads. With cunning they conspire against your people; they plot against those you cherish. "Come," they say,

AMERICA'S 48ᵀᴴ PRESIDENT AND THE MORNING STAR—THE TWO KINGS OF TYRE

"let us destroy them as a nation, so that Israel's name is remembered no more." With one mind they plot together; they form an alliance against you— the tents of Edom and the Ishmaelites, of Moab and the Hagrites, Byblos, Ammon and Amalek, Philistia, with the people of Tyre. Even Assyria has joined them to reinforce Lot's descendants." (Psalm 83:1–8)

If you follow ancestry, you'll discover that the oppressors mentioned in Psalm 83 are ancestors of modern-day Europeans and Arabs. You'll notice this Psalm prophesies the collusion of such people in efforts to vanquish the true people of Israel in entirety. The people of Yehuda (true Jews) were oppressed in Rome, whose Eastern Empire (Constantinople) fell to the Islamic Ottoman Empire, thus becoming Istanbul Turkey. The people of Yehuda (true Jews) later migrated through the Middle East, where they were forced into Islam and slaughtered by Muhammad and his Caliphate who controlled the entire Middle East.

Jews who survived the onslaught kept migrating and made it to northern Africa where a considerable number of them converted to Islam for trade and survival benefits. Those who chose to keep their religion continued marching into the heart of Africa, settling by the Niger River in places known today as Ghana, Benin, Nigeria, Cameroon, and Angola, amongst others. Don't question Yahuah for allowing other races to conquer the true Jews (black people) because it's also written in the scriptures that Yahuah doesn't permit His people to participate in idol worship. Basically, the other nations and races could thrive in their idol worship, but the people of Yahuah (True Israelites and Jews) would always be held captive by these other nations if, and when they chose to worship the gods of those nations. It's that simple, so to those wondering, Africans wouldn't have been subjected to slavery if their ancestors weren't slaves to idols.

The same cycle of events kept happening to Jews who couldn't refrain from worshipping idols and as such were always held in captivity, as seen in the times of Ancient Babylon, Persia, Greece, and

Rome, and then in the modern era, where the descendants of those aforementioned nations came across the seas to enslave them once again. By the time of the transatlantic slave trade, West Africans were immersed in endemic wars where they killed and enslaved each other, offering humans as blood sacrifices to lesser gods. Although the Old Testament culture remained prevalent amongst the people, only a handful of Jews knew Yahuah, for most of them had turned to idol worship. A batch of the few Jews who knew Yahuah were aboard the slave ship named La Amistad, known to have wrestled control from the slavers in 1839. Their tale is immortalized with a few exceptional innuendos, including their frequent chants of "yah, yah, yah," as if exclaiming halleluYah, which means "praise to Yah!"

Hoshea Last King of Israel

In the twelfth year of Ahaz king of Judah, Hoshea son of Elah became king of Israel in Samaria, and he reigned nine years. He did evil in the eyes of the Lord, but not like the kings of Israel who preceded him.

Shalmaneser king of Assyria came up to attack Hoshea, who had been Shalmaneser's vassal and had paid him tribute. But the king of Assyria discovered that Hoshea was a traitor, for he had sent envoys to So king of Egypt, and he no longer paid tribute to the king of Assyria, as he had done year by year. Therefore Shalmaneser seized him and put him in prison. The king of Assyria invaded the entire land, marched against Samaria and laid siege to it for three years. In the ninth year of Hoshea, the king of Assyria captured Samaria and deported the Israelites to Assyria. He settled them in Halah, in Gozan on the Habor River and in the towns of the Medes.

AMERICA'S 48TH PRESIDENT AND THE MORNING STAR—THE TWO KINGS OF TYRE

Israel Exiled Because of Sin

All this took place because the Israelites had sinned against the Lord their God, who had brought them up out of Egypt from under the power of Pharaoh king of Egypt. They worshiped other gods and followed the practices of the nations the Lord had driven out before them, as well as the practices that the kings of Israel had introduced. The Israelites secretly did things against the Lord their God that were not right. From watchtower to fortified city they built themselves high places in all their towns. They set up sacred stones and Asherah poles on every high hill and under every spreading tree. At every high place they burned incense, as the nations whom the Lord had driven out before them had done. They did wicked things that aroused the Lord's anger. They worshiped idols, though the Lord had said, "You shall not do this." The Lord warned Israel and Judah through all his prophets and seers: "Turn from your evil ways. Observe my commands and decrees, in accordance with the entire Law that I commanded your ancestors to obey and that I delivered to you through my servants the prophets." But they would not listen and were as stiff-necked as their ancestors, who did not trust in the Lord their God. They rejected his decrees and the covenant he had made with their ancestors and the statutes he had warned them to keep. They followed worthless idols and themselves became worthless. They imitated the nations around them although the Lord had ordered them, "Do not do as they do."

They forsook all the commands of the Lord their God and made for themselves two idols cast in the shape of calves, and an Asherah pole. They bowed down to all the starry hosts, and they worshiped Baal. They sacrificed their sons and daughters in the fire. They practiced divination and sought omens and sold themselves to do evil in the eyes of the Lord, arousing his anger.

So the Lord was very angry with Israel and removed them from his presence. Only the tribe of Judah was left, and even Judah did not keep the commands of the Lord their God. They followed the practices Israel had introduced. Therefore the Lord rejected all the people of Israel; he afflicted them and gave them into the hands of plunderers, until he thrust them from his presence." (2 Kings 17:1–20)

Allow me to catch my breath from reading the sins of our ancestors who although had the almighty, all-powerful God of all gods walking with them, performing miracles and wonders before their very eyes, still chose to bow before lifeless objects. You'll also see in verse 16 that they worshipped starry hosts, known as sky gods. Now you see why it's impossible for black people to blame Yahuah for the punishment that came upon them. It's also glaring evidence that the ones who suffered such woes prophesied in multiple scriptures are the black people. Israel spent over four hundred years in Egyptian captivity, just as black people spent over four hundred years enduring the transatlantic slave trade. Hence why in chapters 2 and 3 of Revelation, Christ says the Turkic people claiming to be Jews aren't afflicted.

The Jewish imposters went through one faction of suffrage (holocaust) that lasted twelve years in the entire history of mankind, compared to a combined thousands of years black people have spent in captivity, from the time of Moses in Egypt to the era of brutal inhumane slavery in America. Black people remain in the lands they were held captive to date, spreading and multiplying rapidly, quickly going from minority to majority. Unbeknownst to the slavers, black

AMERICA'S 48TH PRESIDENT AND THE MORNING STAR—THE TWO KINGS OF TYRE

people were being gathered in these lands where they were held captive. They'll continue to grow within these nations and despite efforts to subdue additional migration into the western lands, inexplicable things will happen in their favor until the minority become the majority. The Turkic people claiming to be Jews aren't poor either, and they control most of everything today, including the media, banks, and most social media networks. Unlike black people who constitute billions of people across the world, the Turkic people claiming to be Jews amount to just over fourteen million people worldwide.

Identifying black people as the people of Yehuda (Judah) isn't to trigger hatred or incite any animosity. This message is reflective of truth and not intended to rouse any hatred toward any race of peoples. The scripture has clearly detailed that all people are now Yahuah's people through the sacrifice of Christ, who came to redeem not only the people of the race He was not only born into but also to redeem people of other nations that believe in Him. This is why the apostles spoke in tongues during the Pentecost, reversing the curse of Babel, so the gospel of Christ could reach all the ends of the world.

> "I speak the truth in Christ—I am not lying, my conscience confirms it through the Holy Spirit—I have great sorrow and unceasing anguish in my heart. For I could wish that I myself were cursed and cut off from Christ for the sake of my people, those of my own race, the people of Israel. Theirs is the adoption to sonship; theirs the divine glory, the covenants, the receiving of the law, the temple worship and the promises. Theirs are the patriarchs, and from them is traced the human ancestry of the Messiah. God who is over all be forever praised!" What if he did this to make the riches of his glory known to the objects of his mercy, whom he prepared in advance for glory— even us, whom he also called, not only from the Jews but also from the Gentiles? As he says in Hosea: "I will call them 'my people' who

are not my people; and I will call her 'my loved one' who is not my loved one," and, "In the very place where it was said to them, 'You are not my people,' there they will be called 'children of the living God.'" (Romans 9:1–5 and 23–26)

The brevity of this deep scripture reverberates the sanctity of Christ's sacrifice throughout the world. The norm was that Israel was God's chosen people, but that changed through the sacrifice of Christ that reserved salvation, not only for the Jews but also for Gentiles alike. Paul clarifies that Jews, although being from the race considered "inferior," are indeed the true people chosen by Yahuah, to receive the scriptures, and build His temple, and that from their ancestry comes the Messiah. Meaning, *Christ was a black man from the tribe of Yehuda (Judah)*, which is why the color of his extremities is described as "burnished bronze" in the books of Daniel 7 and Revelation 1. The hair texture of God Almighty (ancient of days) and Christ are both likened to the texture of wool, which is known to be the texture of black people's hair. Burnished bronze is a shade of brown, and 'there are several ways to prove the identity of Christ, but I'll set that aside for another time.

Paul goes further to pose a rhetorical question insinuating why Yahuah could've done such, and he referenced scriptures in Hosea to buttress his point. I mentioned at the beginning of this letter that Christ's true name Yahusha was intentionally replaced in the Holy Bible for multiple reasons, and now I've arrived at yet another one. Christ's true name was changed to hide his black identity just because they didn't want to accept a supremely divine human being, coming from the so-called inferior race. This is why they altered Christ's name and ascribed a Roman name (Ioesus) to Him. The alteration of His name plays a significant role in them being able to whitewash His identity. For example, if I want to claim someone was European, and their name is Patel, it would be very difficult to present that case because the name Patel is known to originate from India. So to hide this person's identity from being revealed by their uniquely particular name, I would change their name to something like Aragos, and then

AMERICA'S 48TH PRESIDENT AND THE MORNING STAR—THE TWO KINGS OF TYRE

transliterate it to Lagos. Now you have no way to identify this person is from India, just by their name—and just like that, Mr. Patel has become Lagos.

Hebrews named their children in specific manners that mostly pay homage to Yahuah. This is why you have names like Yehuda, meaning "thanks to Yahuah," Yahusha, meaning Yahuah saves, and so forth. This is somewhat indicative of how Yorubas name their children after Yahuah, whom they call Oluwa (pronounced Oh-luh-wah). So a Yoruba child would be named Oluwafemi meaning "God loves me" or Oluwaseun, meaning "thank God." The Igbo tribe of Nigeria is also named in that manner, although the pronunciations differ, and they specifically had biblical names, prior to when the slavers came to explore Africa in the 1700s. Yorubas and Igbos were among the people of Yehuda who migrated from Rome to the Middle East to West Africa. Of course, we already know slaves were taken from West Africa (Ghana, Nigeria, Angola, and other West African nations), which is why the DNA test results of the descendants of slaves in America all trace significant portions of their genetic makeup back to West Africa. Yes, the bloodline of Christ came from the people of Yehuda, and the people of Yehuda, migrated to West Africa, only to be recaptured as slaves and scattered across Europe as prophesied in the Holy Scriptures for thousands of years ago.

Slavers brought the Holy Bible, but Africans were the ones who had the culture expressed in the Bible. If you read the Old Testament, you'll notice the people of Israel were primarily given customary laws and practices to observe including; naming and circumcision of kids on the eighth day (Genesis 17:10–12, Christ was circumcised, Luke 2:21), paying the dowry of a bride (Exodus 22:16), older sister marrying before the younger sister (Genesis 29:25–26), maintenance of a woman's virginity until marriage, bowing to the ground before adults as a sign of respect (Genesis 19:1, 23:7, and 12, 18:2, 46:2, 2 Samuel 24:20, etc.). Despite centuries of Western influences, these traditions remain prevalent amongst the Yoruba and Igbo tribes of Nigeria to date. The slavers were armed with guns, shackles, and the Holy Bible but had no clue what the contents of the Bible were about, besides the portion that told slaves to obey their masters. They were a bunch of uncircumcised men who worshipped demons but used Christianity to divide and conquer.

It's unfortunate to hear some black people say, "Christianity is the white man's religion," due to their lack of knowledge. The slavers burned any and everything that could've identified the Africans they took as Jews, and they brutally took every bit of the African culture away from the slaves they shipped to their lands. Some of the methods they used are known as "buck breaking," whereas they'd bind a male slave with his pants down and sodomize him while other slaves watched. This buck-breaking practice was something they enjoyed, and it grew into sex farms where white men traveled across plantations raping male slaves for pleasure. These are the same men who claimed to be a superior race, identified as Christians, and called Africans "pagans, Saracens, and subhuman." I plead with the readers of this message to refrain from breeding any hate in their hearts toward any of the truth divulged in this letter.

The gospel I preach is that of peace, and it doesn't call for any hypocrisy. Some Africans enslaved each other and did abominable things to their own women and children long before the slavers came to Africa. Today, African Americans hurt, kill, and destroy each other more than any other race. So before you spring into a malicious rant over things of the past, albeit systematically imposed to date, look in the mirror and become a version of what Christ asks you to be, which is to love your neighbors, and to do unto others what you'd want them to do unto you, regardless of their race, creed, or religion. I'd welcome the descendant of a former slaver who proves to be a true Christian, over a wayward descendant of a former slave who's motivated by evil. This means race should not play a factor in your alliances with people, rather, judge by what they present to be, with great care of course. I'll probably lose a lot of friends and family due to the contents of this letter, but it only means they were never my family to begin with, and I'll quote the scripture for those afraid to lose 'family members' by sharing the gospel of truth.

> While Yahusha (Christ)was still talking to the crowd, his mother and brothers stood outside,

> wanting to speak to him. Someone told him, "Your mother and brothers are standing outside, wanting to speak to you." He replied to him, "Who is my mother, and who are my brothers?" Pointing to his disciples, he said, "Here are my mother and my brothers. For whoever does the will of my Father in heaven is my brother and sister and mother." (Matthew 12:46–48)

The message is loud and lucid. Allow me to inform you also that the people in the geographical space known today as Israel are not the true Israelites, but I'll leave that conversation for later since I must focus on warning America.

I prefaced this letter with warnings of America's impending judgment on April 8, 2024, the same day the nation will witness a total eclipse. I likened this upcoming event to the biblical story of Jonah who preached to Nineveh and their punishment was averted due to their repentance. The King of Ancient Nineveh took the warning seriously and published a decree that mandated the entire nation to repent from evil and observe a fast, down to the animals. Ancient Nineveh was described as an exceedingly great city that took Jonah 3 days to cover on foot, and although America is probably a thousand times bigger than Nineveh, we do have communication facilities that weren't available then, so I hope this letter can make it around in time. The hot spot is Little Egypt in Southern Illinois, so maybe that's comparable in scale to Ancient Nineveh.

Prophecy 3

Southern Illinois is called Little Egypt, and they have several towns named after cities that existed in Ancient Egypt. The entire region pays homage to paganism, and there are a plethora of places and institutions named after or bearing images of Ancient Egyptian gods. Little Egypt has places like Gold Pyramid, Garden of the Gods, witchcraft covens, and so forth. They also have the Southern Illinois Pagan Alliance and a university whose mascot is Horus, the hawk-headed son of Osiris. This state is going to feel the judgment of God through the earthquake. Texas will witness Yahuah's magnificence through a Christian monument, and the Mississippi River will never be the same. The earth will bring forth locusts, and pagan monuments will fall all over America, including the statue of Satan (a.k.a. Statue of Liberty), the Space Needle, obelisks, and many more. Alaska will be devastated, the San Andreas fault line will split, and Oregon will be flooded. The impacts of these effects will trigger tsunamis in Japan, and the beautiful city of Tokyo will be gravely affected. The Yellowstone National Park will experience a volcanic eruption. America's economy will suffer, food shortages will sweep the country, and military personnel will intervene by flying cargo planes of food and supplies to stranded locations. Citizen benefits will be cut off, and riots will ensue. There'll be civil unrest. The US economy will eventually crash, and the value of the dollar will be severely compromised. America must repent and surrender to the warnings of our Creator, for no amount of earthly intelligence can ready any nation for the power Yahuah can exert over the earth He commanded into existence. I advise all Americans to stock their homes with dry foods and water in the event of temporary power

AMERICA'S 48TH PRESIDENT AND THE MORNING STAR—THE TWO KINGS OF TYRE

outages or food shortages. Buy solar-charged light sources with battery-powered options. There may be a forty-day grace from the day of eclipse, meaning the earthquakes happen around the eleventh of May, but be prepared, as these signs will reveal themselves this year, and the seven-year Tribulation will begin a few years afterward.

We live in a different era, and one king, or president, is no longer able to have such influence over its people, but there is hope. I pray America can take this warning and implement some form of repentance from their wicked ways. However, I would be remiss to hold my breath over this because America is built on so many lies and bloodshed, meaning a revelry of the truth and admittance of crimes committed by their higher powers would jeopardize the nation's dominance, and stir anger from within. Anger from the supremacists who will refuse to relinquish their identity of supposedly being supreme, and anger from the disparaged race of suppressed people who would inevitably discover their identity and how their entire existence was whitewashed through devious wickedness. I need America to know that Yahuah calls for your repentance and for you to acknowledge Him as the One True God. The higher powers in America know exactly what I speak of since they are mostly Freemasons, initiated into cults that discuss alchemy, power, and dominance through the lesser gods they serve.

Prophecy 4

The world elites are working on releasing a new disease to reduce world population, like they did with COVID-19. They are creating this disease similarly to how they created and accidentally leaked the COVID virus. For the sake of Yahuah's elect, the plan may not be quite as successful as COVID-19, but efforts will remain to eliminate a significant number of people using evil tactics. The goal of this is to escalate coordinated efforts toward controlling the masses, their behaviors, and ultimately putting power in the hands of a governing body that completely restricts and regulates citizens all over the world. For those unawares, presidents that belong to some elite organizations have been sabotaging the agricultural sector of their own countries, causing food production to decline drastically in favor of importing processed foods. There are several reasons for that, one being the preparation for famines, another being attempts to slowly poison what goes into the bodies of people, and another being an attempt to neutralize the body's alignment with Yahuah by feeding it chemicals in place of organic foods.

Sperm production in males across America has reduced by 50 percent since the 1950s, and this was thoroughly studied by reputable independent facilities. Breast milk production in mothers has declined, causing babies to be reliant on processed formulas. Although stress can be an added factor for some things, please note that plenty of diseases have emerged over the last few centuries of industrialization and reliance on mass-produced, chemical-ridden, alternate-sugared, fast, and glutton-aided foods. Your bodies are intentionally poisoned for profit, leading to an overreliance on drugs that damage other things in your body, while Big Pharma is geared

AMERICA'S 48TH PRESIDENT AND THE MORNING STAR—THE TWO KINGS OF TYRE

to keep organic options off the table. The earth is poisoned in the name of profit, and those who commandeer or profit most from it yell "climate change," which is yet another "opportunity" for them to control and aggrieve citizens as they build wealth for themselves.

Western countries spent centuries polluting the atmosphere through the emissions of their industrialization and polluted the waters around the world by dumping chemicals in rivers and oceans. These illicit dumps polluted waters from Boston Harbor to the Mississippi River, swept into the oceans and across the rest of the world, from the Pacific to Timbuktu. Now these same countries impose sanctions on small developing countries that are operating at a tiny fraction in comparison to them. The Western world elites collude on ways to suppress citizens, clamoring for the need to curb individual emissions, when a few round trips on their private jets or mega yachts produce more pollution than an entire country of cars would produce in a year. Please remember the name Klaus Schaub.

Prophecy 5

President Trump will likely unknowingly lay the groundwork that initiates certain events in the seven-year tribulation period to come. He desperately needs Yahuah for several reasons other than the presidential seat. The president after him, the forty-eighth president of the United States of America, will be the Antichrist or will give power to the Antichrist that'll bring forth the maturity of the seven-year tribulation of the end times (I must be shrewd with my words). There have been attempts to transpose the spirit of a sky god into an American president, and it will be successful at the time of the forty-eight president. Such spiritual reincarnation will occur when CERN's hadron collider ports the spirit of Abaddon the destroyer, from the Abyss. When Abaddon is released, he'll influence the forty-eighth president of the United States to issue a nuclear strike upon two nations, specifically using F-35 planes to drop nuclear warheads. For now, I'm unable to speak on the specific years these things will happen. Before then, the war in Israel will escalate to involve an oil giant, and Israel's attack on such nation will drive the prices of oil to significant heights, causing gas prices to skyrocket over double the current rate.

Prophecy 6

After a quick decisive strike on two emerging world powers located in the East and in the Northern Hemisphere respectively, a global government will be formed with the American president in full control of the entire world, deferring much of the power to a wealthy king of a foreign nation. This global president will commission the full implementation of a one world religion, thus introducing the mark of the beast era. Allow me to articulate with precision that the forty-eighth president of the United States is going to be acting as, or in favor of, the Antichrist of the end times. It is important for you to know that forewarnings are being sent out, and signs are out there for all to behold the impending return of the Messiah. These things will happen within this generation, in about as much time as a tenth of a tenth of God's Day in human time.

If I'm no longer here when these things manifest, let this letter serve as a reminder that our Father in heaven spoke through me, just as He'll continue to do until my time is up. That's why God set my name aside for Himself, to represent His full glory and magnificence, that He indeed is the Living God that lives forever, and I'm one of His true few messengers unafraid of divulging His unadulterated truth. So come what may, I'm ready to live in my faith, speak His truth, be persecuted for, and die proclaiming His name. Many celebrate getting a job at a big corporation, but I jubilate day and night that I was found worthy to work for our Father in heaven. The worldly things are no longer of importance to me, and vanity is obscure before my eyes.

My spiritual eyes are open, and I see evil for what it is. I'm bold enough to look the devil in his face and say, "YAHUSHA REBUKES YOU,

SO TO HELL WITH YOU," knowing I only owe reverence to the One and Only Almighty God who is worthy of my adulation, and to His true Son who paid the ultimate price so that all who believe in Him can be saved. The hands of modern church institutions may be tied because of their interdependence on the government, and affiliation with worldly organizations or individuals who benefit them, but I speak freely because I depend on no man, need nothing from no man, and I'm totally reliant on provisions attributed to me by my Father in heaven. My ancestors ate manna and died, but I eat from the Living Bread, and I drink from the Living Waters, so my soul shall live forever and ever.

America's Idols and Pagan Monuments

Let those who have ears listen to the warnings and foretelling of what's to come. For unsuspecting citizens, please pay attention to the signs that exist all over this nation of America, and you'll see that it is indeed paying homage to the same ancient gods whom nations like Ancient Egypt and Babylon were built upon. For example, a pair of obelisks called Cleopatra's needles were moved from Egypt to the Western world. One was transported to London, and the other was transported to the United States, nestled specifically in New York's Central Park. The one in New York is paired with two locally made obelisks that are aligned meticulously over several miles to match the constellation pattern called Orion's belt. It's noteworthy that several men died while transporting these Obelisks that weigh more than some skyscrapers.

The one in America was mounted in 1881, a year that saw America witness two significant earthquakes, with two more in the subsequent year, making a quadruple event on the New Madrid beltline, just three months apart. These earthquakes happen to be the greatest in the history of America—talk about blood sacrifice to the pagan gods. London would also have a wave of disasters after erecting their Cleopatra's needle in January of 1878. These disasters include 'the Princess Alice disaster' which claimed over seven hundred lives, the "wood pit disaster," which claimed over two hundred lives, and the "Prince of Wales colliery explosion," which claimed 268 lives, among others.

The vessel towing the Cleopatra needle that went to London was caught in a storm at Biscay Bay, causing six men to die in rescue attempts. The Obelisk was then mounted on the Thames Embankment, flanked by two bronze sphinxes which are also pagan monuments. When the Cleopatra needle cornerstone was laid in New York, over nine thousand cult members of the Freemasons marched through the city, signifying how big of a deal it was to this cult of sky god worshippers. The Obelisk in New York is covered with inscriptions giving glory to Amun Ra for all the fortune he bestowed upon their nation.

Inscriptions on the New York obelisk

"The crowned Horus Bull of Victory Arisen in Thebes." "The lord of the Vulture and Uraeus crowns Prolonged as to kingdom, Even as the sun in the heavens. By Tum Lord of On begotten, son of his loins, who hath been fashioned by Thot, Whom they created in the great-temple With the perfections of their flesh, Knowing what he was to perform, Kingdom prolonged through ages, King of Upper and Lower Egypt Men-kheper-ra (Thûtmosis Il).

Loving Tum, the great god, With his cycle of divinities, Who giveth all life stay and sway, Like the sun forever. Who smiteth the rulers of the nations-Hundreds of thousands; In as much as father Ra Hath ordered unto him Victory against every land, Gathered together; The valor of the scimeter In the palms of his hands To broaden the bounds of Egypt; Son of the Sun, Thûtmosis I, Who giveth all life forever. Glorified of Osiris Like the Sun life-giving forever.

The chosen of Ra, the golden Horus Rich in years, great in victory, Son of the Sun, Ramses II, who came forth from the womb Life giving like the Sun forever." To receive the crowns of Ra; fashioned was he to be the sole ruler…"

You clearly see what these obelisks are all about—giving praises, mainly to the sun god in whose honor they're erected. So let it be known that when you hear America say, "In God We Trust," the god in that phrase is Lucifer, and I'll prove it in its entirety.

William H. Vanderbilt paid a hefty price to transport Cleopatra's Needle to New York, and the Vanderbilt family also financed Grand Central Station in New York. The ceiling of Grand Central Station has murals of constellation clusters, including that of Orion, whose belt is aligned perfectly with the constellation in the sky. The obelisk from Ancient Egypt (Cleopatra's Needle) is paired with two other obelisks in New York, one of which is positioned at the entrance of St. Paul's Chapel on Broadway, with the third being in Worth Square. All three New York obelisks are lined up in the manner of Orion's Belt just like the pyramids of Giza. Up in the skies, Orion's belt points at Sirius, which translates in Egyptian mythology to mean Osiris is in constant pursuit of his lover, Isis. The Orion's Belt formed by the obelisks in New York points at Lady Liberty (The Statue of Liberty) strategically placed in honor of Isis. The Statue of Liberty also represents Libertas, the Roman goddess of freedom. These things are monuments to the gods worshipped by this nation. America must repent by getting rid of these monuments, as that's one of the many ways to avert Yahuah's judgment. Although I pray day and night for mercy, I won't hold my breath in anticipation of this nation's repentance for her roots of evil descend deep into the abyss.

America's original obelisk, located in Washington, DC, was the tallest building in the world back when it was dedicated in October of 1888, after taking about forty years to be completed. Why are these European nations obsessed with obelisks that give glory to the sun god? Why do they sacrifice human lives and undertake laborious endeavors to build these monuments? The answer is that they operate at the direction of these gods whom they're slaves to.

It just occurred to me that the fourteenth missing part of Osiris that remained unrecovered was his phallus (penis), which was eaten by a fish. So allow me to point out that each obelisk you see is a giant erection pointed toward the sun to compensate for Osiris's missing phallus. That paints a horrid picture to reckon with, considering many men who think themselves intelligent are forking out tons of money, laboring over, and sacrificing human lives to erect a giant penis to a sky god. Wow!

Pardon my gentle reminder that two devastating earthquakes occurred in the United States after the giant phallus of Osiris was floated across the oceans and erected in New York's Central Park. After the two earthquakes of 1881, two equally devastating earth-

AMERICA'S 48TH PRESIDENT AND THE MORNING STAR—THE TWO KINGS OF TYRE

quakes followed at the top of the following year. The 1881 earthquakes occurred northeast of Arkansas, in a location that would be later known as Memphis, Tennessee. Memphis was named after the capital of Ancient Egypt, governed by a group of gods like Iris, Osiris, Seth, and Amun-Ra. The 1882 earthquakes occurred in the Missouri Bootheel region where a town called New Madrid was completely destroyed. New Madrid's origin comes from the Muslim age when Emir Muhammad I of the Umayyad Caliphate built a fortress by the river of the Iberian Peninsula. The surrounding waters are where the name 'Madrid' comes from, meaning "water fountain" or "stream," suggestive of the fortress built next to the water. In this instance, we see another location in America paying respects to another not-so-ancient nation that's governed by the pagan Muslim god.

Islam and Muhammad
The Second Beast of the End Times

The Muslim god is called Allah, and his prophet is Muhammad, whose followers formed the Islamic Caliphates. For those unawares, Allah was a pagan god worshipped by the Arabs, long before Prophet Muhammad was born. The only thing Muhammad did was to break the other stone gods and establish Allah as the only one to be worshipped, right in the same shrine where they used to worship 360 pagan gods, including Allah. Muhammad preaches that Christ is just a prophet, and that's a red flag, for whoever preaches such an Antichrist, as seen in the Holy Scriptures.

> Dear children, this is the last hour; and as you have heard that the antichrist is coming, even now many antichrists have come. This is how we know it is the last hour. They went out from us, but they did not really belong to us. For if they had belonged to us, they would have remained with us; but their going showed that none of them belonged to us. Who is the liar? It is whoever denies that Jesus is the Christ. Such a person is the antichrist—denying the Father and the Son. No one who denies the Son has the Father; whoever acknowledges the Son has the Father also. (1 John 2:18–19 and 22–23)

AMERICA'S 48TH PRESIDENT AND THE MORNING STAR—THE TWO KINGS OF TYRE

These verses reveal that some false religions went out from the established premise of Christianity by hitching their claims to the Holy Bible, all while claiming that Christ is just a prophet. Christ was prophesied for thousands of years, through dozens of prophets, and He fulfilled every single one of those prophesies, so it's quite ironic that one man who was prophesied by absolutely no one can claim Christ as his equal. Muhammed claims he saw the same angel (Gabriel) who brought the message of Christ's birth, telling him to go from a new religion that claims Christ isn't the true Son of our Father in heaven. That's not only absurd, but also there's no one to corroborate such a story besides the one person who tells it, which in this generation is called a "trust me, bro" story. The Antichrist is whoever says that Christ isn't the Son of Yahuah. So if your religion states such, I'm sorry, but you worship a false god, and your prophet is one of the prophesied antichrists. I don't doubt that these prophets are indeed visited by an Angel, but the question is, what angel?

> For such people are false apostles, deceitful workers, masquerading as apostles of Christ. And no wonder, for Satan himself masquerades as an angel of light. It is not surprising, then, if his servants also masquerade as servants of righteousness. (2 Corinthians 11:13–14)

It's important to note that any angel who opposes the message in the Holy Bible is not of Yahuah but of Satan. Once again, we see how another religion hitches its ride on the wave of the Holy Bible but opposes it at the same time. Don't take my word for it though, allow me to quote certain scriptures in the Quran (inspired writings of Allah), just so you can see how Satan rears his ugly head in there to unsuspecting followers of the religion.

> In the sight of Allah on the Day of Resurrection and the worst person and target of His wrath would [be] the person who is called Malik al-Am-

lak (the King of Kings) for there is no king but Allah." (Sahih Muslim 2143b)

It's apparent that Allah clearly hates Christ, who is known as the King of kings. Allah is ready to battle Christ on the Day of Resurrection, which is seen in the Holy Bible as the day Christ defeats the beast.

> I saw heaven standing open and there before me was a white horse, whose rider is called Faithful and True. With justice he judges and wages war. Coming out of his mouth is a sharp sword with which to strike down the nations. "He will rule them with an iron scepter." He treads the winepress of the fury of the wrath of God Almighty. On his robe and on his thigh he has this name written: king of kings and lord of lords. Then I saw the beast and the kings of the earth and their armies gathered together to wage war against the rider on the horse and his army." (Revelation 19:11–12, 15–16 and 19.)

This is the war Muhammad speaks of, so it's clear to see that Muhammad is an Antichrist, and Allah is the beast. The Quran clearly says Allah is going to battle Christ, the King of kings. This isn't a guess, and I'll prove further how the Quran focuses obsessively on disproving the divinity of Christ, presenting Him to be just another man like Muhammad.

> Then they schemed (against the Messiah), and Allah countered their schemes by schemes of His own. Allah is the greatest deceiver. when Allah said, ""O Jesus, indeed I will take you and raise you to Myself and purify you from those who disbelieve and make those who follow you [in submission to Allah alone] superior to those who

AMERICA'S 48ᵀᴴ PRESIDENT AND THE MORNING STAR—THE TWO KINGS OF TYRE

> disbelieve until the Day of Resurrection. Then
> to Me is your return, and I will judge between
> you concerning that in which you used to differ."
> (Quran 3:54–55)

If reading the Quran almost gives you a concussion, you're not alone. Anyways, the referenced message is once again geared directly against Christ, and it's riddled with claims that the Christian God is Allah, whilst also saying in the same breath that Allah hates Christ, and that Allah will fight against Christ in the battle of Armageddon. Muhammad and his message of Allah presents the most glaring evidence of an antichrist and the beast described in the Holy Scriptures.

PLEASE NOTE THE QURAN ALSO STATES THAT ALL MUSLIMS ARE GOING TO HELL.

> "And there is none among you who is not to
> arrive at hell. This means that everybody—be
> he a believer or an infidel—will go across Hell.
> However, this does not mean that they would go
> to stay in it; they would only go across it. But
> even if the word means "entry"," then the pious
> believers on entry into hell will feel no discom-
> fort because the fires will cool down and will do
> no harm to them". (Quran 19:71)

Ladies and gentlemen, that is the promise of Islam, that all their believers will enter hell. That is a guarantee and lurid promise that's articulately expressed for what it is. Once again, you see Allah (Satan) declare the truth as he must do, to present his case before Yahuah. Satan is the accuser, and he's like a conniving salesman who hides all the bad clauses of a contract in the fine print. Once you sign the document, you're bound by its contents before the Judge, and it doesn't matter if you read the content or not. It doesn't matter if you understood what you signed up for or not. It's not about what's fair, just as you can't buy a car as-is then complain you didn't know it'd have issues. By purchasing a car as-is, it means the seller informed you that he or she waives responsibility for any problems, so please pay attention to the promise Islam makes and take it at face value. If you follow a religion that causes you to take a mark of the beast (I'll explain later), or to denounce Christ as the true son of Yahuah, you will surely go to hell, just as Allah declared to you in his fine print called the Quran.

This is why it was mandated by Muhammad that the Quran must be read in the original Arabic language, even when shared to non-Arabic-speaking people. I grew up in Lagos, Nigeria, where people didn't speak Arabic but would learn the Shahadah (the mark of the beast which I'll explain later), and a few lines of Arabic they'd recite forever. The Quran was a mystery book they couldn't read, so the warnings in the fine print of Allah were kept safely tucked away from them. Many have perished around the world without knowing, and all I can do is attempt to save those that are still redeemable.

Now here's Allah's promise of what Muslims should expect in the Islamic heaven:

> "A happy life is reserved for the righteous. gardens and vineyards. Girls with big breasts, their age, and jugs full. No ill speech will they hear therein or any falsehood. This is your Lord's reward, a generous gift. (Quran 78:30–40)

> "We forged the uri of Paradise in a special way. And we kept them pure virgins. These are reserved for right-wing people". (Quran 56:35–38)

> The messenger of Allah said, "Everyone that God admits into paradise will be married to 72 wives; two of them are [virgins] and seventy of his inheritance of the female dwellers of hell. All of them will have libidinous sex organs and he will have an ever-erect penis." (Hadith 4337)

AMERICA'S 48TH PRESIDENT AND THE MORNING STAR—THE TWO KINGS OF TYRE

Prophet Muhammad said, "Every man who enters paradise shall be given 72 (seventy-two) virgins; no matter at what age he had died when he is admitted into paradise, he will become a thirty-year-old, and shall not age any further. A man in paradise shall be given virility equal to that of one hundred men" (At-Tirmidhi p138).

> But Allah's chosen servants (shall be spared this woeful end). For them awaits a known provision, a variety of delicious fruits; and they shall be honored in the Gardens of Bliss. They will be seated upon couches set face to face; a cup filled with wine from its springs, will be passed around to them; white, sparkling (wine), a delight to the drinkers. There will neither be any harm in it for their body nor will it intoxicate their mind. Theirs shall be wide-eyed maidens with bashful, restrained glances, so delicate as the hidden peel under an egg's shell. (Quran 37:40–49)

It's quite glaring that Islam's version of heaven is a promise of lust, eternal erections, drunkenness, a host of virgins to each man, and other salacious obsessions. If the promise of heaven is centered around men having bewitchingly beautiful women to pick from, does that mean Muslim women are only meant to serve as sex slaves in their heaven? The former sinful-minded version of me would've loved this type of paradise, but I'm awakened in spirit and dead to lust. However, I assume it does make a great recruitment speech for their warriors and suicide bombers who believe they're awaited in heaven by a plethora of virgins suited for their enjoyment. I once wondered how they got young men to expire themselves in a violent instant, but I understood after reading the Quran. The religion permits them to have as many women as they can afford to marry on earth, even going as far to allow prostitution, something they refer to as Mut'a—a paid temporary arrangement married or unmarried Muslim men can have with any strange woman they desire to have sex with. I wouldn't fault anyone who cites the sexual provisions and promises that are made to Muslims in heaven and on earth, as why young men flock to Islam or die fighting for it.

> O People of the Book (Jews and Christians)! Commit no excesses in your religion: Nor say of Allah aught but the truth. Christ Jesus the son of Mary was (no more than) a messenger of Allah, and His Word, which He bestowed on Mary, and a spirit proceeding from Him: so believe in Allah and His messengers. Say not "Trinity": desist: it will be better for you: for Allah is one Allah: Glory be to Him: (far exalted is He) above having a son. To Him belong all things in the heavens and on earth. And enough is Allah as a Disposer of affairs. (Quran 4:171)

In Arabic, this verse literally says, "Kalimatuhu wa Ruhunminhu," which means "Christ is the word of Yahuah and a spirit from Him." It goes further to say, "Wa'kalimatuhu alqaha ila maryama wa'roohun minhu," which translates to mean, "Yahuah's word was cast upon Mary." This confirms Christ is the word of God, a part of God, who was already existing in spirit, and then cast upon Mary to be born in flesh. A portion of the verse speaks the truth, then goes on to say Allah doesn't have a son, so whoever believes in the Trinity should desist from doing so. Here once again you see the clandestine nature of Satan, putting in his fine print that Christ is indeed of Yahuah, and one with Yahuah. He establishes this truth and then goes on to confuse the reader with lies. Now if a salesman surreptitiously includes in his/her contract that a car is faulty and liable to break down at any time, he/she can also butter the car up by claiming it to be like new. It's up to the reader to analyze the document in its entirety and discern what portion of the contract to believe, but if you're fooled into signing a terrible agreement, it's your loss, and you must deal with whatever consequences arise.

Yahuah and Allah are not the same. Yahuah has a son, Allah doesn't. Yahuah has prophets, and Muhammad is not one of them.

AMERICA'S 48TH PRESIDENT AND THE MORNING STAR—THE TWO KINGS OF TYRE

Yahuah mentions all His prophets in the Holy Scriptures, and Muhammad is not referenced to be any of His prophets. So one man (Muhammad) cannot rise out of nowhere and lead many to believe the entire foundation of the Holy Bible that existed before his ancestors is false, all while basing the validity of his own religion on that same Bible. The Holy Bible comprises of hundreds of characters that existed thousands of years before Muhammad, and everything prophesied in the Bible are proven to be historically accurate and true.

Muhammad was nothing but a soldier, just like Constantine, who saw an opportunity to rise into and maintain power, by using a popular religion. Constantine was a pagan who hitched his chariot onto Christianity, using it to conquer and then formed the pagan Catholic religion afterward. Muhammad was a pagan who hitched his horses onto Christianity, by using it to establish validity for his Islamic religion, which he used to conquer and then implemented among his peoples. Catholicism syncretized Roman paganism into Christianity, whilst Islam syncretized Arab paganism into a religion their prophet roped around Christianity. Both Catholicism and Islam are antichrist establishments the devil has used to win billions of souls in his favor.

Muhammad's Prophetic Privileges

> O Prophet, We have made lawful for you your wives whose bridal dues you have paid, and the slave-girls you possess from among the prisoners of war, and the daughters of your paternal uncles and paternal aunts, and the daughters of your maternal uncles and maternal aunts who have migrated with you, and a believing woman who gives herself to the Prophet and whom he wants to take in marriage. (O Prophet), this privilege is yours alone to the exclusion of other believers. We know well what restrictions We have imposed upon them as regards their wives and those whom their right hands possess, (and have exempted you from those restrictions) that there may be no constraint upon you. Allah is Most Forgiving, Most Merciful. (Quran 33:50, 87–90)

Well, that's one unholy grail of privileges chalked up to a prophet. Once again, we see a dynamic of sexual compulsions, lustful fascinations, and nympholepsy in the religion of Islam, whereas Allah makes provisions of many women to his devotees. In this instance, Allah bestows on his beloved prophet Muhammed, special encumbrances to take female slaves, any Muslim woman that gifts herself to him, the daughters of his own family, and as many other women as he wants, all without an ounce of constraint. Muhammed and his Islamic Caliphates were recorded in history to divide women captives among themselves as spoils of war, acting homogenous to pirates who live for days where they rob, kill, and share the booty.

> They wish that you should disbelieve, as they have disbelieved, and thus you become all alike. So, do not take friends from among them unless they migrate in the way of Allah. Then if they turn away, sieze them, and kill them wherever you find them... (Quran 4:89)

Here you see Allah advising Muslims to kill all who refuse to migrate toward him. We're specifically focused on Christianity, a religion based on the teachings of Christ, so let's compare Muhammad's method of spreading Allah's gospel to Christ's method of spreading Yahuah's gospel.

> These twelve Yeshuah sent out with the following instructions: "Do not go among the Gentiles or enter any town of the Samaritans. Go rather to the lost sheep of Israel. As you go, proclaim this message: 'The kingdom of heaven has come near.' Heal the sick, raise the dead, cleanse those who have leprosy, drive out demons. Freely you have received; freely give. If anyone will not welcome you or listen to your words, leave that home or town and shake the dust off your feet." (Matthew 10:5–8 and 14)

There's a glaring difference here as you see Muhammad preach violence, whilst Christ on the contrary is all about spreading peace and healing through His apostles. It's also noteworthy that in Luke 10:18, another group of seventy-two people whom Christ had sent out to spread His gospel returned, saying, "Yahusha, even the demons submit to us in your name." There is no power in the name of Muhammad, and he never sent people out to do any good but to conquer, enslave, and oppress anyone who didn't proclaim Allah as

63

their god, with the joint assertion that he (Muhammad) is Allah's prophet. There are over a hundred commands in the Quran calling for the murder of those who refuse a conversion to Islam. Basically, Muhammad, under the command of Allah waged war on anyone who wouldn't accept the mark of the beast. Muhammad married a six-year-old girl named Aisha and was verified to have been having intercourse with her at the tender age of nine. If that's not pedophilia, then I don't know what is, but as Christ says, "By their fruits you shall know them," meaning their deeds will show you who they truly are.

The Kaaba is a shrine in Mecca, Saudi Arabia, where 360 stone idols were worshipped during the era of pre-Islamic Arab paganism. When Muhammad conquered Mecca, he broke all other stone idols in favor of "the black stone," which was already venerated for worship by the pagan Arabs. This black stone was fastened to the corner of the Kaaba, and the shrine became a "holy site" for all Muslims. Over time, a mosque was built around the Kaaba, and it has since been declared the holiest site in the Islamic religion. All Muslims are required to direct their prayers to that black stone, under the belief they're praying in the direction of the temple. Muhammad is a mimic who not only tries to be Christ-like but fashioned Islam after another religion that existed long before his time. The religion I speak of is Zoroastrianism, and a close look into it will help any reader understand that Muhammad essentially committed the worst, but most successful, plagiarism of all time. Zoroastrianism was founded by one man (Zarathustra) who claimed to have received divine visions, prompting him to form a new religion—Muhammad copied. Zoroastrianism's prophet is the only prophet to the god of the religion—Muhammad copied. Zoroastrianism is a monotheistic derivative of ancient Mesopotamian religion—Muhammad copied. Zoroastrianism separated from Proto-Indo-Iranian paganism, just as Islam is a monotheistic derivative of ancient Arab paganism. Hence, Zoroastrianism and Islam are fraternal twins born over two thousand years apart, yet difficult to distinguish in doctrine, based on their striking resemblances.

Similarities between Zoroastrianism and Islam

They're both founded by one 'prophet' who claimed divine angelic visitation. They both originated in Arab regions. They both order their worshippers to pray five times a day, facing the specific location of their temples when praying. They're ordered to pray only in the original languages of their founders (Arabic and Avestan). Both prophets had night visions and terrors that are indicative of demonic possession. They both pray in relation to the movement of the sun, which is indicative of sun worship. They both believe in a respite stage after death, and that each person must cross through a bridge—yet another striking resemblance to the belief of ancient Egyptians who worshipped a sun god named Amun Ra. They both mention beautiful maidens in heaven. They both mention that a spiritual scale will weigh their deeds, with a middle abode destined for whoever's scale isn't tipped toward either good or bad. Muhammad died from sickness, while Zarathustra was killed in an altercation. Christ died for our sins, rose from death, and ascended to heaven in full view of all who were present.

Ancient Babylonians worshipped in relation to the sun and moon, so it's easy to deduce that Islam and Zoroastrianism pay reverence to the sun by way of their worship. The Islamic symbol is a crescent moon and a star, showing the reverence they ascribe to celestial beings. Muhammad asked all Muslims to make at least one trip to the Kaaba so they can kiss the same black stone that was venerated as a god, worshipped by his ancestors. That certainly fits the criteria of idol worship. Muhammad formulated Islam and adopted pre-Islamic pagan beliefs including worship at the Kaaba shrine, worship of the black stone, incorporation of 'jinn (spirits), and so forth.

In Quran 34:50, Muhammad was commanded by Allah to say: "If (even) I go astray, I shall stray only to my own loss. But if I remain guided, it is because of the Inspiration of my Lord to me. Truly, He is All-Hearer, Ever Near (to all things)." Sigh, it's disconcerting to know 'there are billions of people 'who have been led astray (past and present) by the teachings of someone that was clearly possessed by the spirit of Satan. Anyone who reads the Quran can clearly see that it's an Antichrist campaign filled with nothing but slander unto Christ, truthful admissions in certain parts about the divinity of Christ, encouragement of violence, the view of women as sex slaves, and the fate of hell that awaits all followers of Islam.

Muhammad said a voice called to him, "O Muhammad, you are the messenger of God, and I am the Angel Gabriel." Through this claim and by name-dropping almost all the characters in the Holy Bible, Muhammad had the world thinking Christianity and Islam are governed by the same God. Such attempts to amalgamate both religions by lying on Angel Gabriel, and peddling a drove of misconceptions through the Quran have led plenty of souls astray. Galatians 1:7–8 would address such purveyors of falsehood, stating, "Evidently some people are throwing you into confusion and are trying to pervert the gospel of Christ. But even if we or an angel from heaven should preach a gospel other than the one we preached to you, let them be under Yahuah's curse!"

Back to America

I apologize for the lengthy delineations, but I, too, am caught off guard by the pace at which the Holy Spirit is flowing through me in terms of these revelations. I'm typing off memory and inspiration, so everything included here is all at the direction of my Father in heaven. I took a break to pray about the weightiness of these things, asking if some could be removed for the sake of limiting my exposure to criticism and to focus all attention on America's impending disaster, but the message is His, and I'm only a vessel of conveyance. This letter happens to be an all-encompassing message that unbeknownst to me is intended to shake the foundations of people's beliefs, just as the foundations of the addressed nation are about to be shaken. Anyways, allow me to take you on a journey that explains the world of otherworldly entities, how they play significant roles in affecting us, and the judgment to befall them, including all humans who follow their ways.

> God presides in the great assembly; he renders judgment among the "gods": "How long will you defend the unjust and show partiality to the wicked? Defend the weak and the fatherless; uphold the cause of the poor and the oppressed. Rescue the weak and the needy; deliver them from the hand of the wicked. "The 'gods' know nothing, they understand nothing. They walk about in darkness; all the foundations of the earth are shaken. "I said, 'You are "gods"; you are all sons of the Most High. 'But you will die like

mere mortals; you will fall like every other ruler." (Psalm 82:1–7)

"What are mortals, that they could be pure, or those born of woman, that they could be righteous? If God places no trust in his holy ones, if even the heavens are not pure in his eyes, how much less mortals, who are vile and corrupt, who drink up evil like water! (Job 15:15–16)

Though you already know all this, I want to remind you that Yahuah at one time delivered his people out of Egypt, but later destroyed those who did not believe. And the angels who did not keep their positions of authority but abandoned their proper dwelling—these he has kept in darkness, bound with everlasting chains for judgment on the great Day. In a similar way, Sodom and Gomorrah and the surrounding towns gave themselves up to sexual immorality and perversion. They serve as an example of those who suffer the punishment of eternal fire. (Jude 1:5–7)

Yahuah is angry with all nations; his wrath is on all their armies. He will totally destroy them, he will give them over to slaughter. Their slain will be thrown out, their dead bodies will stink; the mountains will be soaked with their blood. All the stars in the sky will be dissolved and the heavens rolled up like a scroll; all the starry host will fall like withered leaves from the vine, like shriveled figs from the fig tree". (Isaiah 34:2–4)

In the referenced scriptures, you'll see that Yahuah is clearly angry at the rebellious gods who continually use men to lead the world astray. He reprimands them because they go around wreaking

AMERICA'S 48TH PRESIDENT AND THE MORNING STAR—THE TWO KINGS OF TYRE

havoc thinking they're wise when they're indeed foolish. Yahuah further makes it known that although they are gods, they will be subjected to the same fate as mortal men. For this, I coined the phrase, "Foolish gods lead foolish men to foolish deeds." The sons of God rebelled against Yahuah, except His one True Son, Yahusha. Many lack understanding of how things work in the spiritual hierarchy established by Yahuah, hence why Christ was accused of blasphemy for citing His divinity, citing His oneness with God Almighty.

> Why then do you accuse me of blasphemy because I said, 'I am God's Son'? Do not believe me unless I do the works of my Father. But if I do them, even though you do not believe me, believe the works, that you may know and understand that the Father is in me, and I in the Father." (John 10:36–38)

Imagine for a moment that Yahusha, God the Son, manifested in flesh to dwell amongst men, and to show them the way, yet many hated Him and sought His prosecution. This proves you need God's wisdom and the guidance of the Holy Spirit to see, hear, feel, know, and recognize what's of God Almighty, and what's of lesser gods. I'll proceed to use scriptures to prove the power and influences of these gods here on earth.

> Then he continued, "Do not be afraid, Daniel. Since the first day that you set your mind to gain understanding and to humble yourself before your God, your words were heard, and I have come in response to them. But the prince of the Persian kingdom resisted me twenty-one days. Then Michael, one of the chief princes, came to help me, because I was detained there with the king of Persia. Now I have come to explain to you what will happen to your people in the future, for the vision concerns a time yet to

come." So he said, "Do you know why I have come to you? Soon I will return to fight against the prince of Persia, and when I go, the prince of Greece will come; but first I will tell you what is written in the Book of Truth. (No one supports me against them except Michael, your prince.) (Daniel 10:12–14, and 20–21)

You see in those verses that Angel Gabriel was sent by Yahuah to deliver a message to Daniel, but he was held hostage by the Prince of Persia, who is the sky god that ruled the land of Persia. Archangel Michael had to come from heaven to free Angel Gabriel from the spiritual detainment he was subjected to. Angel Gabriel also referenced that the Prince of Greece was yet to come, foretelling that another sky god would soon raise the Greeks to be the dominating empire in the world. Angel Gabriel ends his message by saying he only gets help from Archangel Michael whenever he's here on earth. These lesser gods were once higher-ranking celestial beings in the heavens, which is why they're powerful enough to detain Yahuah's messenger, so imagine the preeminence they have over mere humans. Now allow me to prove the divinity of Christ and how he's been our God from the Old Testament, till He manifested in flesh into the New Testament, and continues to be here for us thereafter, till this day!

God's Angel to Prepare the Way

"See, I am sending an angel ahead of you to guard you along the way and to bring you to the place I have prepared. Pay attention to him and listen to what he says. Do not rebel against him; he will not forgive your rebellion, since my Name is in him. If you listen carefully to what he says and do all that I say, I will be an enemy to your enemies and will oppose those who oppose you. My angel will go ahead of you and bring you into the land of the Amorites, Hittites, Perizzites, Canaanites, Hivites and Jebusites, and I will wipe them out. Do not bow down before their gods or worship them or follow their practices. You must demolish them and break their sacred stones to pieces. Worship the Lord your God, and his blessing will be on your food and water. I will take away sickness from among you, and none will miscarry or be barren in your land. I will give you a full life span. (Exodus 23:20–26)

Remember I apprised you to the transfiguration of Christ's true name in the scriptures by a group of conniving humans who sought to deceive the world. In some instances, they also used "The Lord" in replacement of Christ's true name, and "the LORD" to replace Yahuah's true name. It doesn't matter what version of the western bible you're reading because all translations were completed under the strict supervision of the Roman Catholic Church who crowned all monarchs like King Charlemagne of France, and King James of England. Everything that was passed onto mankind through the Western world, including religion, education, sciences, and philosophies were all supervised and approved by the Papal office of the Roman Catholic Church, which served as the controlling body of European countries.

Armed with this knowledge, you can see the referenced verses in Exodus 23 reveal that God Almighty (Yahuah) appointed His Son, Yahusha, who they referred to as an angel, to lead and guide Israel from Egypt to the promised land. You'll notice in verse 20, Yahuah says the people must not rebel against him for he will not forgive their rebellion. Yahuah also says, "My name is in him","" which is reminiscent of when Christ said in John 5:43, "I come bearing my father's name but you do not accept me." No angel bears the name of Yahuah, so the 'angel' in Exodus 23 is Christ. Exodus 23:25 truly says, "Worship Yahusha your God, and his blessings will be on your food and water," but this time, they replaced Christ's name with "the Lord." Following my spiritually guided decipherment of these name-change-nuances might seem a bit exhaustive to simple minds, but stick with me while I prove this in entirety. I quoted the promise of Yahuah in Exodus 23, to send Israel 'an angel' that bears His name. Now I'll show you the deeds and authority of that 'angel.'

> "The angel of the Lord went up from Gilgal to Bokim and said, "I brought you up out of Egypt and led you into the land I swore to give to your ancestors. I said, 'I will never break my covenant with you, and you shall not make a covenant with the people of this land, but you shall break down their altars.' Yet you have disobeyed me. Why have you done this? And I have also said, 'I will not drive them out before you; they will become traps for you, and their gods will become snares to you, When the angel of the Lord had spoken these things to all the Israelites, the people wept

AMERICA'S 48TH PRESIDENT AND THE MORNING STAR—THE TWO KINGS OF TYRE

aloud, and they called that place Bokim. There they offered sacrifices to the Lord." (Judges 2:1–5)

I hope this sparked a light of excitement within you in the realization of the truth. There you see the angel Yahuah promised to lead Israel into the promised land now being referred to as the angel of the Lord. I already proved the angel of the Lord to be Christ at the beginning of this letter, but I'll reiterate and reinforce such a claim. In the quoted verses I just shared from the book of Judges, you'll see 'the angel of the Lord' reprimand Israel for breaking their covenant with him. He goes on to pass judgment unto the Israelites in accordance with the forewarnings of Yahuah. The glaring point is that the angel of the Lord led Israel, reprimanded them, and passed judgment upon them, based on the commands expressed by Yahuah in Exodus 23. Christ executed Yahuah's commands in the Old Testament in Spirit form, before manifesting in flesh to execute additional commands in human form. Hence why He said, *"These words you hear are not my own; they belong to the Father who sent me..." and "I love the Father and do exactly what my Father has commanded me" (John 1:24 and 31).*

> By day the Lord went ahead of them in a pillar of cloud to guide them on their way and by night in a pillar of fire to give them light, so that they could travel by day or night. Neither the pillar of cloud by day nor the pillar of fire by night left its place in front of the people. (Exodus 13:21–22)

> Then the Lord said to Moses, "Why are you crying out to me? Tell the Israelites to move on. Raise your staff and stretch out your hand over the sea to divide the water so that the Israelites can go through the sea on dry ground..." Then the angel of God, who had been traveling in front of Israel's army, withdrew and went behind them. The pillar of cloud also moved from in front and

stood behind them, coming between the armies of Egypt and Israel. Then Moses stretched out his hand over the sea, and all that night the Lord drove the sea back with a strong east wind and turned it into dry land. The waters were divided, and the Israelites went through the sea on dry ground, with a wall of water on their right and on their left... Then the Lord said to Moses, "Stretch out your hand over the sea so that the waters may flow back over the Egyptians and their chariots and horsemen... Moses stretched out his hand over the sea, and at daybreak the sea went back to its place. The Egyptians were fleeing toward it, and the Lord swept them into the sea." (Exodus 14:15, 19–22, and 26–27)

Then Moses and the Israelites sang this song to the Lord: "I will sing to the Lord, for he is highly exalted. Both horse and driver he has hurled into the sea. (Exodus 15:1)

The Lord reigns, let the nations tremble; he sits enthroned between the cherubim, let the earth shake. Great is the Lord in Zion; he is exalted over all the nations. Let them praise your great and awesome name—he is holy. *The King is mighty*, he loves justice...Moses and Aaron were among his priests, Samuel was among those who called on his name; they called on the Lord and he answered them. He spoke to them from the pillar of cloud... (Psalm 99)

Ladies and gentlemen, all mentions of the Lord, angel of the Lord, and angel of God are titles they used in replacing "Yahusha," which is the true name of Christ. The one exception is when they used an angel of the Lord to describe Angel Gabriel. In other scriptures,

AMERICA'S 48ᵀᴴ PRESIDENT AND THE MORNING STAR—THE TWO KINGS OF TYRE

Yahuah's name was replaced with titles like, the LORD, Sovereign God, and God Almighty. When Angel Gabriel brought the news of Christ to Mary, here's what the KJV states:

> And the angel said unto her, Fear not, Mary: for thou hast found favour with God. And, behold, thou shalt conceive in thy womb, and bring forth a son, and shalt call his name "JESUS. (Luke 1:30–31)

Now we know that's a blatant lie for many reasons, first being that the letter J didn't exist until only a few hundred years ago. *Jesus* is a transliteration of *Ioesus*, which is a Greek name they ascribed to Christ. Neither Ioesus nor Jesus is a Hebrew name. So to boldly state that Angel Gabriel mentioned the name *Jesus* shows you the Europeans colluded to change the identity of our savior. I'll gather my points with additional scriptural references.

> Then the Lord spoke to Job out of the storm. He said: "Who is this that obscures my plans with words without knowledge? Brace yourself like a man; I will question you, and you shall answer me. "Where were you when I laid the earth's foundation? Who marked off its dimensions? When I made the clouds its garment and wrapped it in thick darkness, when I fixed limits for it and set its doors and bars in place, when I said, 'This far you may come and no farther; here is where your proud waves halt'? "Have you ever given orders to the morning, or shown the dawn its place, that it might take the earth by the edges and shake the wicked out of it? The earth takes shape like clay under a seal; its features stand out like those of a garment. "Have you journeyed to the springs of the sea or walked in the recesses of the deep? Have the

gates of death been shown to you? Have you seen the gates of the deepest darkness? Have you comprehended the vast expanses of the earth? Tell me, if you know all this. "What is the way to the abode of light? And where does darkness reside? Can you take them to their places? Do you know the paths to their dwellings... "Have you entered the storehouses of the snow or seen the storehouses of the hail, which I reserve for times of trouble, for days of war and battle? What is the way to the place where the lightning is dispersed, or the place where the east winds are scattered over the earth? Who cuts a channel for the torrents of rain, and a path for the thunderstorm, to water a land where no one lives, an uninhabited desert, to satisfy a desolate wasteland and make it sprout with grass? Does the rain have a father? Who fathers the drops of dew? From whose womb comes the ice? Who gives birth to the frost from the heavens when the waters become hard as stone, when the surface of the deep is frozen? "Can you bind the chains of the Pleiades? Can you loosen Orion's belt? Can you bring forth the constellations in their seasons or lead out the Bear with its cubs? Do you know the laws of the heavens? *Can you set up God's dominion over the earth?* (Job 38:1–38 condensed)

You see, this is Christ speaking to Job. He established the premise of His professions in the first person, stating, "I did this," "and that, and all that." He then posed a question to Job, saying, "Can you set up God's dominion over the earth?" Job had questioned Yahuah, asking for a mediator who could present his case before God Almighty. Well, he received a long speech from Yahuah's mediator (Christ) on how man's intelligence is highly limited in comparison to

AMERICA'S 48TH PRESIDENT AND THE MORNING STAR—THE TWO KINGS OF TYRE

Yahuah's. It was Christ who appeared to Job, but you wouldn't know because they changed His name to "the Lord." Well, the main point is that Christ basically made it known that He created everything at the behest of Yahuah, and there's proof of that.

The Word Became Flesh

> In the beginning was the Word, and the Word was with God, and the Word was God. He was with God in the beginning. Through him all things were made; without him nothing was made that has been made. In him was life, and that life was the light of all mankind. The light shines in the darkness, and the darkness has not overcome it.
>
> —John 1:1–4

Christ is the word of God, and He created everything you see on earth, at the direction of Yahuah, which is why He's God to us, as we live in His precious project that took seven thousand years to create. I say seven thousand years because a thousand days unto man is like a day unto God (2 Peter 3:8). Now you can see there's a lot more to life than what most make of it. There's a lot to spirituality, and 'there are plenty of forces in control of humans all over the world who continue to live within the confines of the devil's control. The world as we know it is corrupted by all the evil entities I've discussed at length, and the wicked rulers of great nations orchestrate their will in exchange for temporary gain and dusty statues that serve their souls no purpose once their time on earth is finished. These rulers of men foolishly believe they can outsmart God Almighty based on the knowledge and alchemy given to them by the fallen angels, sky gods, and corrupt celestial beings. Pitch your tent under Christ for only He has power in the heavens and on earth—even the demons knew Him while He was here.

AMERICA'S 48TH PRESIDENT AND THE MORNING STAR—THE TWO KINGS OF TYRE

When Yahusha arrived at the other side in the region of the Gadarenes, two demon-possessed men coming from the tombs met him. They were so violent that no one could pass that way. "What do you want with us, Son of God?" they shouted. "Have you come here to torture us before the appointed time?" (Matthew 8:28–29)

Yahusha Sends Out the Seventy-Two

After this the Lord appointed seventy-two others and sent them two by two ahead of him to every town and place where he was about to go. He told them, Heal the sick who are there and tell them, 'The kingdom of God has come near to you.' "Whoever listens to you listens to me; whoever rejects you rejects me; but whoever rejects me rejects him who sent me." The seventy-two returned with joy and said, *"Lord, even the demons submit to us in your name." He replied, "I saw Satan fall like lightning from heaven. I have given you authority to trample on snakes and scorpions and to overcome all the power of the enemy; nothing will harm you.* However, do not rejoice that the spirits submit to you, but rejoice that your names are written in heaven." At that time Jesus, full of joy through the Holy Spirit, said, "I praise you, Father, Lord of heaven and earth, because you have hidden these things from the wise and learned, and revealed them to little children. Yes, Father, for this is what you were pleased to do. (Luke 10:1, 9, and 16–21)

Please note they once again replaced Christ's true name with "Lord" and that you'll never see a mention of his true name anywhere in the scriptures. Anyways, you'll notice a few glaring things in the books of Matthew and Luke quoted above—the

AMERICA'S 48TH PRESIDENT AND THE MORNING STAR—THE TWO KINGS OF TYRE

most important being that Christ has power over all principalities and powers. The demons knew who He was and influenced men to get rid of Him, without reckoning that He submitted Himself as the Sacrificial Lamb, to pay for sin once and for all. Christ's sacrifice was so that Satan, the accuser no longer has anything over us. If they had known His death was to redeem our souls in perpetuity, they wouldn't have crucified Him.

Prior to the manifestation of Yahusha in the flesh, a physical temple and High Priests were needed to make sacrifices for the atonement of our sins. Christ became our High Priest, the temple, and the eternal sacrifice. He took our claim to redemption away from the hands of corrupt men and became our direct medium (the mediator that Job desperately pleaded for) to God. According to the law that governs the entire universe, the sacrifice Christ made was the only way to redeem mankind from sin—for sin came into the world through man's corruption, and sin had to leave the world through man's perfection. No man born of flesh would've been able to live a perfect life and that's why Christ had to leave His throne in heaven to dwell amongst the lowliest of men on earth, in perfection, sinless, blameless, yet persecuted and killed with wicked devices.

These simple premises are asinine to those blind in spirit, for the secrets of Yahuah elude "wise" people who rely on earthly wisdom and are revealed unto those who seem to be nobodies. Christ established His authority over the heavens, the earth, and all the spirits living within both abodes. He even references being present when Satan was cast out of the Heavens, something which was done IN HIS NAME, as seen in Revelation 12:

> Then war broke out in heaven. Michael and his angels fought against the dragon, and the dragon and his angels fought back. But he was not strong enough, and they lost their place in heaven. The great dragon was hurled down—that ancient serpent called the devil, or Satan, who leads the whole world astray. He was hurled to the earth, and his angels with him. Then I heard a loud

> voice in heaven say: "Now have come the salvation and the power and the kingdom of our God, and the authority of his Messiah. For the accuser of our brothers and sisters, who accuses them before our God day and night, has been hurled down. They triumphed over him by the blood of the Lamb and by the word of their testimony; they did not love their lives so much as to shrink from death." (Revelation 12:10–11)

I hope you're now abreast that Lucifer and his angels were defeated by Archangel Michael and his angels, who triumphed over him by the blood of the Lamb and by His name. There's power in the blood and in the name of Yahusha. This also lets you know that the accuser who presents cases against us before our God has been defeated by the blood sacrifice of the Lamb, such that whoever pleads His blood shall be forever free from Satan's claim to take their soul. Hence why it's important to live your lives carefully and to surrender yourself to He who paid an expensive price for your body. Nobody would doubt Christ being God if His name wasn't trickily replaced several times throughout the Bible. There wouldn't be a bone of contention amongst His true people if His true identity wasn't altered and whitewashed into the European semblance sold around the world. I also struggled with understanding why Christians were required to worship a man, for so I thought, until I realized Christ isn't a man, but in fact our God from the Old Testament, manifested in flesh AS A BLACK MAN, in the New Testament and died to redeem not only His race, but the entire world. Here's a final scripture on the dynamic of God the Father and His Son, for whoever still struggles with understanding.

> But Christ has indeed been raised from the dead, the firstfruits of those who have fallen asleep. For since death came through a man, the resurrection of the dead comes also through a man. For as in Adam all die, so in Christ all will be

made alive. But each in turn: Christ, the first-fruits; then, when he comes, those who belong to him. Then the end will come, when he hands over the kingdom to God the Father after he has destroyed all dominion, authority and power. For he must reign until he has put all his enemies under his feet. The last enemy to be destroyed is death. For he "has put everything under his feet." Now when it says that "everything" has been put under him, it is clear that this does not include God himself, who put everything under Christ. When he has done this, then the Son himself will be made subject to him who put everything under him, so that God may be all in all." (1 Corinthians 15:20–28)

Yahuah installed Christ as God until all evil has been conquered and the scepter is handed back to Yahuah.

A Moment of Full Transparency

I've presented cogent evidence to convey God's truth in this letter, which, to my surprise, evolved into somewhat of a theological dissertation. I must declare that I do not have any formal training in theology; I did not attend any pastoral schools, nor did I learn any of this from another human. I prayed fervently and didn't relent until I heard Yahusha's voice, followed by messages of confirmation from unexpected individuals like my music producer. This made me seek God further, so I got baptized, kept praying, and fasted for forty days, including many days without food or water (the secret they took out of most Bible versions that omit verse 21 in Matthew chapter 17). I've been filled with the Holy Spirit who continues to strengthen me, and I was assigned an angel of teaching who has taken me on plenty of rides that feel like I'm immersed in a whirlwind of information.

At the inception of my journey, I chickened out a few times and would ask for it to stop, but I soon matured in spirit and handle it much better, although it's still a lot. There's a world out there that's completely unfathomable even by the wildest imaginations, and I'm honored to get glimpses of it. My spiritual journey started when I heard God speak to me in September of 2023, and the most prominent thing I heard Him say was, "I gave you the gift of words, how dare you not use it to exalt me?" I understood from that moment that I was called to be a Soldier of Yahuah, but I was very reluctant to preach. I tried bargaining to make some gospel songs or do something along the lines of my comfort zone, but God said, "David was a musician and a prophet." I kept struggling with the idea and expressed vehemently to my wife that I didn't want to preach, acting

AMERICA'S 48TH PRESIDENT AND THE MORNING STAR—THE TWO KINGS OF TYRE

like I had a choice. It took me about two months to finally come to grips with it, and here I am, ruffling the feathers of all the mighty eagles that rule the world. Oh well, I know He who called me is greater than He who is in the world, so I march onward.

The Final Segment

"Though you already know all this, I want to remind you that Yahusha at one time delivered his people out of Egypt, but later destroyed those who did not believe. And the angels who did not keep their positions of authority but abandoned their proper dwelling—these he has kept in darkness, bound with everlasting chains for judgment on the great Day. In a similar way, Sodom and Gomorrah and the surrounding towns gave themselves up to sexual immorality and perversion. They serve as an example of those who suffer the punishment of eternal fire. In the very same way, on the strength of their dreams these ungodly people pollute their own bodies, reject authority and heap abuse on celestial beings. But even the archangel Michael, when he was disputing with the devil about the body of Moses, did not himself dare to condemn him for slander but said, "The Lord rebuke you!" Yet these people slander whatever they do not understand, and the very things they do understand by instinct—as irrational animals do—will destroy them. Woe to them! They have taken the way of Cain; they have rushed for profit into Balaam's error; they have been destroyed in Korah's rebellion. These people are blemishes at your love feasts, eating

AMERICA'S 48TH PRESIDENT AND THE MORNING STAR—THE TWO KINGS OF TYRE

with you without the slightest qualm—shepherds who feed only themselves. They are clouds without rain, blown along by the wind; autumn trees, without fruit and uprooted—twice dead. They are wild waves of the sea, foaming up their shame; wandering stars, for whom blackest darkness has been reserved forever. Enoch, the seventh from Adam, prophesied about them: "See, the Lord is coming with thousands upon thousands of his holy ones to judge everyone, and to convict all of them of all the ungodly acts they have committed in their ungodliness, and of all the defiant words ungodly sinners have spoken against him"." These people are grumblers and faultfinders; they follow their own evil desires; they boast about themselves and flatter others for their own advantage." (Jude 5–16)

Allow me to fully dissect this hefty message in what stands as the last book before the book of judgment, known as Revelation. The message is prefaced with the fact that Christ led people out of Egypt and destroyed those who didn't believe in Him. It goes on to say that angels (the watchers) who didn't keep their positions of authority over men were bound until the day of judgment (as narrated in the book of Enoch). Sodom and Gomorrah are then mentioned to highlight how sexual immorality and perversion condemn those who practice it to hell, along with those who refuse the authority of Christ and serve celestial beings (and sky gods) instead. Verse 9 emphasizes the power in the name of Yahusha once again, affirming that even Archangel Michael uses His name to contend with the devil, just as he used it to defeat Lucifer in Revelation 12 (quoted earlier).

Verse 10 admonishes the ignorance of all who slander the name of Christ due to their lack of understanding, and Verse 11 will be broken into parts to help understand the magnitude of the three names that were mentioned:

Balaam's Error

Balaam's error refers to those who lead God's chosen people to sin by offering them food sacrificed to their gods. Christ addresses this in *Revelation 2:14: Nevertheless, I have a few things against you: There are some among you who hold to the teaching of Balaam, who taught Balak to entice the Israelites to sin so that they ate food sacrificed to idols and committed sexual immorality.*

> They will be paid back with harm for the harm they have done. Their idea of pleasure is to carouse in broad daylight. They are blots and blemishes, reveling in their pleasures while they feast with you. With eyes full of adultery, they never stop sinning; they seduce the unstable; they are experts in greed—an accursed brood! They have left the straight way and wandered off to follow the way of Balaam son of Bezer, who loved the wages of wickedness. (2 Peter 2:13–15)

That's another verse showing reproach for Balaam's error, which is articulated in all three scriptures (Jude 1, Revelation 2, and 2 Peter 2) to indicate a disdain for those who popularized sexual immorality and tricked the chosen people of God into eating food sacrificed to idols (pagan holidays). I don't know how I strategically arrived at these junctures in the letter, but they all line up with the message to America and why judgment is coming upon this woeful nation before God. The Holy Spirit appears to be on autopilot through my mind and fingers. Dear Americas and the People of Yehuda (black people), please *stop* participating in pagan feasts just because you've normalized them. Valentine's Day, Halloween, Easter, Christmas, New Year on January 1 (dedicated to Roman god Janus whom January is named after), Labor Day (dedicated to Roman goddess Maia), St. Patrick's Day, and so forth.

Korah's Rebellion

Korah's rebellion sends a warning about the fate to befall those who collude against true servants of Yahuah. Korah and a group of Israelites gathered themselves to challenge Moses who was acting on behalf of God. They mustered accusations as though Moses was at fault for leading them out of Egypt, and this caused dissension in the camp. I'll let the scriptures narrate the fate of Korah and the rebellious men.

> Then Moses said, "This is how you will know that the Lord has sent me to do all these things and that it was not my idea: If these men die a natural death and suffer the fate of all mankind, then the Lord has not sent me. But if the Lord brings about something totally new, and the earth opens its mouth and swallows them, with everything that belongs to them, and they go down alive into the realm of the dead, then you will know that these men have treated the Lord with contempt." As soon as he finished saying all this, the ground under them split apart and the earth opened its mouth and swallowed them and their households, and all those associated with Korah, together with their possessions. They went down alive into the realm of the dead, with everything they owned; the earth closed over them, and they perished and were gone from the community. (Numbers 18:28–33)

Once again, I've somehow come full circle to scriptural references that resonate with America's impending judgment. Here also, you see the earth responds to the commands of its Creator and is indeed alive as I alluded to at the beginning of this letter.

The Way of Cain

"The way of Cain" represents a refusal to observe what's right before God, by choosing to do what's convenient in accordance with one's personal estimations. Meaning, you refuse to follow the rules set forth in the scriptures and convince yourself that Christ will accept you just the way you are. If you follow the way of Cain, you're basically expecting God to accept the things He condemns, just because you acknowledge Him. It also represents those who bring condemnation on righteous souls by intentionally leading them to destruction, just as Cain woke his brother up and led him to his death.

> You snakes! You brood of vipers! How will you escape being condemned to hell? Therefore I am sending you prophets and sages and teachers. Some of them you will kill and crucify; others you will flog in your synagogues and pursue from town to town. And so upon you will come all the righteous blood that has been shed on earth, from the blood of righteous Abel to the blood of Zechariah son of Berekiah, whom you murdered between the temple and the altar. Truly I tell you, all this will come on this generation. (Matthew 23:33–36)

That's a quote from Christ condemning those who refuse the Gospel of truth and subject the righteous messengers to slander, suffering, scrutiny, or systemic oppression. So whoever condemns anyone for speaking the truth is lost to "the way of Cain," and the blood of all righteous souls will be an inheritance to be emptied upon their heads. It's ironic I mentioned earlier in this letter that judgment was coming in this generation, and now the Holy Spirit has led me to a scripture where Christ says, "All this will come on this generation," in a chapter that precedes His prophecies of end times, just as the book (Jude) which led to this segment precedes the end-time book of Revelation.

Wow! I had to take a prayer break after typing out that last word, realizing the full picture that got painted at the inception of this final segment. I had chills, my mouth was open, and I fell into a trance and projected into a scene at the end of days, envisioning the horror to befall so many people in denial of the truth. God is speaking, Yahusha is raising the saints persecuted in His name and readying the angels for His second coming. These kinds of men think they can outsmart the King of kings, but they're in for a rude awakening. I must gather myself and finish this mission, so here I go. Sigh!

Back to Matthew chapter 23 where I left off. As mentioned by Christ in verse 33, hell is also reserved for rulers who implement a system that encourages the suppression of the truth, systematically persecutes those who preach the truth, and for the benefactors who indulge in the fruits of the sinful "way of Cain." For example, the American government legalized same-sex marriages during the forty-fourth administrations, and it led to an unprecedented acceleration in the rate of sexual perversions in America, and all over the world through America's confounding influences. The result is a slew of pronouns and laws that normalize and even legalize things that were unerringly categorized as mental challenges or demonic possessions, just a few decades ago. This leads to the giant in the room—one of the worst sins condemned in the Holy Bible; the sins of abnormal sex and sodomy, named after the infamous story of Sodom and Gomorrah.

For any who doubt the story of Sodom and Gomorrah, I encourage you to watch the YouTube Video of Joel Kramer's "Expedition Bible" page titled "Sulfur balls of Sodom and Gomorrah." In this video, he visited the actual location of Sodom and Gomorrah, and thousands of Sulphur balls, as described in the Holy Bible. Joel Kramer torches some of these balls and they all burn out with potency, despite being immersed in the Dead Sea for over four thousand years. Here we are at the final section of what presents to be the longest letter ever!

LGBTQ2 + Phenomena

Alert: God makes no mistakes, so stop believing you were born with a confused sexual orientation. Evil spirits do possess infants, even from the womb, so understand that your condition stems from one or many evil spirits that have afflicted you at some point. It's also impermanent and there's a cure for the derision that has overcome your mind and body. The solution isn't to surrender to the grips of the wayward sex demons confusing your mind, neither is it in the hands of psychologists or sex change surgeons, as they've led many to think. The solution resides with Christ who condemns such demons and has the authority to cast and bind them, as documented in many of His New Testament miracles.

Sodomy, homosexuality, and same-sex relations are some of the most accursed sins in the Bible, but they've been normalized by the Western world who continue to prop, promote, encourage, and divulge this to a wide audience, ranging from infancy to adulthood. The United States relentlessly promotes this LGBTQ2+ agenda in infant cartoons, all the way to teenage shows and adult movies. You can barely turn on a movie, show, or listen to a song without hearing the gospel of sexual perversions in America, aiding and abetting one of the devil's favorite sins. There are dozens of scriptures condemning these behaviors, but people enslaved to "the way of Cain," "Balaam's error'," and "Korah's rebellion" have tip-toed around the condemnation of this phenomena and skedaddled with their own version of Christ's gospel.

The favorite line of the supposed Christ-loving LGBTQ2+ folks is "Christ said come as you are." I don't know what Bible they got that from, or what scriptures they tailored into such, but let it be

AMERICA'S 48TH PRESIDENT AND THE MORNING STAR—THE TWO KINGS OF TYRE

known that although Christ is merciful and open to whoever wants to change, He does not condone those who force their own unrealistic ideologies into His Church.

> Or do you not know that wrongdoers will not inherit the kingdom of God? Do not be deceived: Neither the sexually immoral nor idolaters nor adulterers nor men who have sex with men nor thieves nor the greedy nor drunkards nor slanderers nor swindlers will inherit the kingdom of God. (1 Corinthians 6:9–10)

> We also know that the law is made not for the righteous but for lawbreakers and rebels, the ungodly and sinful, the unholy and irreligious, for those who kill their fathers or mothers, for murderers, for the sexually immoral, for those practicing homosexuality, for slave traders and liars and perjurers—and for whatever else is contrary to the sound doctrine. (1 Timothy 1:9–10)

> Because of this, God gave them over to shameful lusts. Even their women exchanged natural sexual relations for unnatural ones. In the same way the men also abandoned natural relations with women and were inflamed with lust for one another. Men committed shameful acts with other men, and received in themselves the due penalty for their error. (Romans 1:26–27)

> In a similar way, Sodom and Gomorrah and the surrounding towns gave themselves up to sexual immorality and perversion. They serve as an example of those who suffer the punishment of eternal fire. (Jude 1:7)

Marriage should be honored by all, and the marriage bed kept pure, for God will judge the adulterer and all the sexually immoral. (Hebrews 13:4)

Do not have sexual relations with a man as one does with a woman; that is detestable. (Leviticus 18:22)

There were even male shrine prostitutes in the land; the people engaged in all the detestable practices of the nations the Lord had driven out before the Israelites. (1 Kings 24)

Flee from sexual immorality. All other sins a person commits are outside the body, but whoever sins sexually, sins against their own body. Do you not know that your bodies are temples of the Holy Spirit, who is in you, whom you have received from God? You are not your own; you were bought at a price. Therefore honor God with your bodies. (1 Corinthians 6:18–20)

There's more scripture I could quote, including the instance in the book of Judges 19 where sexual immorality led to an internal war among the Israelites. However, I think the point has been made with enough references, and I am amiss as to where the LGBTQ2+ pastors got their doctrines of the gospel from. They adorn their pulpit, seeping with abjection, with an adulterated version of God's covenant, which they turned into a flag. What a shame! This is all coming from a place of love and a burning passion to help save these fellow humans of mine whom the Holy Spirit won't allow me to gloss over. I tried to avoid this topic, but here I am, and I'll share my personal story as well, so everyone out there can infer hope toward dealing with their afflictions.

AMERICA'S 48TH PRESIDENT AND THE MORNING STAR—THE TWO KINGS OF TYRE

I, too, was once a slave to perversions like masturbation and having sex with multiple women for fun. I had sex with multiple women at once, and I resented the idea of marriage as a young man because I felt it'd deprive me of having many options. Now I realize that I was afflicted with evil spirits that continually used my body to fulfill their own satisfactions, while also leading me further away from Yahuah. So when I condemn sexual perversions, please know that I've been there, and I know how it feels natural, while there's nothing natural about it. Yahuah cured my insatiable appetite for a variety of women, despite it presenting as a normal thing among men, so it's not hard for Him to purge the spirit of homosexuality or gender confusion, which is clearly abnormal. Addicts convince themselves they're "just like that," forgetting there was once a time they didn't even know of the things they're addicted to. Alcohol, marijuana, cocaine, and all sorts of things were all foreign to you at some point, but how come they're impossible to do without? I shared a very personal truth about myself because I want people to understand that I come from a place of sincerity, not condemnation. So if I sound harsh, it's because such a tone is needed to wake people up from this sugarcoated, cotton candy gospel the megachurches are preaching for the sake of profit or because they don't want to hurt feelings. I'd rather hurt your feelings and save your soul than pacify you and watch you burn in hell later.

When Mary Magdalene was a slave to prostitution, Christ cast seven powerful demons out of her, and she went on to be one of His devout, righteous followers. When Christ saved the adulteress from persecution (John 8), He told her to "sin no more." I say this to show that there's hope, but only in redemption and a total separation from your sinful ways. Grace does expire eventually, and many will unfortunately wait until it does before taking necessary action. You can be delivered from homosexuality and other sexual perversions, I guarantee it.

The United States is the spokesperson for this condemned behavior. Howbeit that one nation can influence the entire world with such obscenity, going so far as imposing sanctions on nations that refuse to be inebriated with their concoction of eternal death. America disguises itself as a nation built on the Christian God but openly endorses, supports, and coerces institutions into implementing abominations the Christian God is against. I must reiterate; the rate of gender confusion has skyrocketed since the forty-fourth administration was used to implement same-sex marriages in America. In less than ten years, kids identifying as the opposite sex or claiming gender neutrality has gone up by almost 20 percent. Now they have Environmental Social Governance (ESG) scores for corporations that rate them based on how much they endorse and promote the LGBTQ+ community, and/or other agendas the world elites wish to promote. What this means is that giant corporations are strong-armed into joining the campaign of spreading the LGBTQ+ message all over the world. I was joyous in 2008, without realizing they sometimes use our kind to rally behind someone they're using to fulfill the will of Satan.

What we're witnessing from America is what Nimrod did during the Tower of Babel era. I knew not of this concept prior to the inception of this letter, but I just receive divine understanding that the world is being united in one common language, the English language. This coordination toward one world globalization is masterminded by a nonpresidential leader from a country in west central Europe, whose native language isn't English but speaks it fluently albeit with a distinct accent. His name is Klaus Schaub, the harbinger of Germany's fourth Reich.

The future American president to assume the Oval Office in 2029 will be mentored by this West Central European with ties to a previous world war. They're forming massive political alliances, world economic bodies, and all sorts of agendas to the control the masses, and make the world a better place, because they supposedly know best. World Economic Forum (WEF) is the strategic body behind economic reforms and coordinated efforts to bring about "the great reset," to take ownership away from citizens, and to install one man as a global, military-styled ruler with control over much of the world's assets.

The name of this organization (WEF) used to be European Management Forum and that tells it yet another Western coalition to control the world by distributing the land amongst themselves,

AMERICA'S 48TH PRESIDENT AND THE MORNING STAR—THE TWO KINGS OF TYRE

at a price (Daniel 11:39), just like they did during the transatlantic slave trade, but this time, their citizens won't be exempt from slavery. The slogan they're trying to imprint on people's minds is that, "You'll own nothing and be happy." That's straight from the notes of Karl Marx, a German political theorist (just like the founder of WEF) who believes in taking all ownership away from the masses, so they can be controlled accordingly.

Prophecy 7

The seven-year tribulation period commences soon, and construction of the One World Religion temples in Jerusalem and New York will be completed between 2028 and 2029, after Russia has been eliminated based on their foiled Arab coalition attempt to crush the nation of Israel. I won't say when the midpoint of the tribulation is, but be aware that rules will be implemented to have people all over the world acknowledge this one world religion to be the true form of worship. Hence the mark of the beast will be introduced. I'll stop the prophecy here and focus on the devil's mark.

Most people know about the mark of the beast but are unaware of the seal of God. The devil is a copycat, and you'll notice that he finds a way to fashion everything he does in semblance to Yahuah's methods. This helps him create confusion and division all over the world, making people doubt the originality of something they seem to have come across elsewhere. If you hear stories that bear similarities to each other, at some point, you'd be confused as to whose story is true or which one preceded the other. The devil has successfully operated this way for so long, and we see its effects whenever you hear people say there were other gods that did what Christ did prior to his time, or that the story of a virgin giving birth to a god already existed prior to Christ.

Well, the first of its kind was once again with Nimrod who impregnated his mother (Semiramis) before his death. When Semiramis found out she was pregnant, she came up with an idea to claim she was impregnated by the spirit of Nimrod who was deified after his death. Hence, her child from the pregnancy (Tammuz) was coined to be a divine being, which is why they revered him as a god.

AMERICA'S 48TH PRESIDENT AND THE MORNING STAR—THE TWO KINGS OF TYRE

This shows you how intelligently foolish the world leaders are, and how they're able to sway the unsuspecting masses into greater stupidity. Anyway, I must inform you about the mark of God.

> These commandments that I give you today are to be on your hearts. Impress them on your children. Talk about them when you sit at home and when you walk along the road, when you lie down and when you get up. Tie them as symbols on your hands and bind them on your foreheads". (Deuteronomy 6:6–8)

> This observance will be for you like a sign on your hand and a reminder on your forehead that this law of the Lord is to be on your lips. For the Lord brought you out of Egypt with his mighty hand". (Exodus 13:9)

The instructions quoted in Deuteronomy were passed unto the Israelites after Yahuah gave them commandments to live by. I quoted similar instructions in Exodus, which was given after Israelites were instructed to observe the feast of Yahuah. Most Christians don't know of this feast, much less take steps to observe them, but we know and celebrate feasts of pagan gods. Well, now you see what it takes to bear the mark of God, which is to live by His commands and embody His will. Yahuah is basically telling us to have His laws imprinted on our minds and evident in all we do, to the best of our ability. That also alludes to "the fear of God," for if you fear Him, you'll refrain from wickedness and immorality. Now let's see the mark of the copycat devil in Revelation 13.

> The dragon stood on the shore of the sea. And I saw a beast coming out of the sea. It had ten horns and seven heads, with ten crowns on its horns, and on each head a blasphemous name. Then I saw a second beast, coming out of the

earth. It had two horns like a lamb, but it spoke like a dragon. It exercised all the authority of the first beast on its behalf, and made the earth and its inhabitants worship the first beast, whose fatal wound had been healed. And it performed great signs, even causing fire to come down from heaven to the earth in full view of the people. The second beast was given power to give breath to the image of the first beast, so that the image could speak and cause all who refused to worship the image to be killed. It also forced all people, great and small, rich and poor, free and slave, to receive a mark on their right hands or on their foreheads, so that they could not buy or sell unless they had the mark, which is the name of the beast or the number of its name". (Revelation 13:1, 12–13, 15–17)

At the time, Revelation was written (around AD 96), it served as a revelry of what was to unfold in the future. That future is now, almost two thousand years later. You see the mark of God was given in the beginning portion of the scriptures, but the mark of the best manifests at the end. Please note that just as the mark of God is a thing of the mind, the mark of the beast *will not* be a literal mark on anyone's foreheads or arms. Now although there are derivates of the beast's mark that I won't expand on for now, it's important to pay attention to verses 15 through 17 of Revelation 13. These verses let you know that a system will be implemented to force people into accepting the mark, which would ultimately be for survival.

For instance, the government will make provisions for people who accept the one world religion to have certain privileges and people will sell their souls just to engage in normal activities. Whoever accepts their rules, has accepted their mark! Simply put. They'll implement a system through technology, that requires people to register, to prove one's conformity to their one world religion. You will be restricted from doing basic things that everyday life is dependent

AMERICA'S 48TH PRESIDENT AND THE MORNING STAR—THE TWO KINGS OF TYRE

upon unless you ascribe to their program. You have been warned. If you must denounce your faith in Christ to get by, that's the mark being imposed on you. Do not renounce the mark of Yahuah in exchange for the mark of the beast.

Christ said it best in Matthew 10:28, "Do not be afraid of those who kill the body but cannot kill the soul. Rather, be afraid of the One who can destroy both soul and body in hell." Remain steadfast in your testimony to Christ our savior. Suffer and die in testimony of His name if need be, for you shall be raised unto everlasting glory with the Saints. Many will take the mark of the beast to spare themselves from the temporary pain, only to be condemned to eternal suffering. I plead with you, to remain firm and resistant. Below are how the marks of the beasts have been introduced in the past.

Roman Catholic Church Inquisition Era

The Catholic Inquisition was a timeframe whereby true Christians (and true Jews) were forced to take the mark of the beast by renouncing their own faith in place of pagan-infused Catholicism. Hence why I referred to the Roman Catholic Church as the first beast as seen in Revelation 13. Whoever refused to adopt Catholicism as the true form of worship was tortured, maimed, and burned alive. As such, millions of people claimed to Catholic converts (taking the mark) while few remained fervent in their testimony to Christ. *Once the veil is removed from your eyes, you'll see the world for what it is and realize that the temporarity promised by men isn't worth losing one's soul for eternity.*

Islamic Caliphate Era

There was a time when the Islamic Caliphate controlled about a quarter of the world's population. Non-Muslims in their regions were persecuted and enslaved, whilst kings of many nations, including African kings converted to Islam for trade benefits. Just like the Roman Catholic Church, the Islamic Caliphate made people pronounce their pagan faith as the true religion in exchange for their lives. Devout followers of both religions are known to have a rosary (or tasbih) wrapped around their right hands to prove their alignment with the faith, and devout Muslims have a literal mark pressed on their forehead from praying in accordance with the Quran. These are the marks of the beasts referenced in Revelation 13. Catholicism is the first beast, and Islam is the second beast. You have been warned!

Many truths have eluded the world for over two thousand years, tucked away in the fifty-three-miles-long vault at the bottom of the Devil's workshop called the Vatican—the site of the unholy Roman Catholic Church. Through their systematic oppression and suppression of the true People of Yehuda, the Hebrew language went extinct but miraculously came back into existence—being the only language in the world to have ever been extinct with no speaking survivors left, and somehow resurged. Other truths have emerged after thousands of years, like the actual name of Christ discovered by other people, and the phrases used to hide Christ's identity in scriptures, that was revealed to me.

We know the names of all these lesser gods whose identities have been placed on our tongues with how they're woven into our daily vocabulary. Months, days, weeks, holidays, and planets are named after lesser gods or their festivals. They all worship the same gods who bear different names across all civilizations, just like Thor is the god of thunder to the Norse, also known as Zeus, the god of thunder to the Greek, also known as "Jupiter's god of thunder to the Romans, also known as Sango to the Yorubas, also known as Indra to the Indians, known as Baal to the Canaanites, as Amun to the Egyptians, and also as Taranis to the Celtics.

These gods are real and celebrated by their worshippers who in turn glorify them before unsuspecting masses through movies, shows, a literary works. Their 'idols' reside in almost every home because our children are obsessed with these 'superheroes.' You'll be surprised to know that most English words have roots, prefixes, and suffixes that make you pronounce the name of their gods unsuspectingly. For example, Pan is a Greek god that half goat, half man, and he's the god of fear, which is why his name is used for words like PANic, PANdemic, PANdemonium, PANtheon, PANgea, and in cartoon characters like Peter PAN.

Other words that pay homage to lesser gods in the English vocabulary include Nymphomaniac (Nymphos), Aphrodisiac (Aphrodite), Atlas (a Titan), Typhoon (father of monsters), Erotic (Eros, who focused on physical love, not emotional), Cupid (who makes incompatible people sexually attracted to each other), Hermes, Protean, Mentor (that's who Olympus left his son to), Tantalize (Tantalus), Achilles (after Achilles), Cereal (god of wheat), Echo, Jovial, Nemesis, and so forth. The English language is riddled with the names of gods and formulated in honor of them. This isn't to necessarily discourage you from the verbiage you understand but mainly to let you know how they've immersed us into paying homage to their gods, all whilst they intentionally hid the name of Yahuah, the Almighty God.

America's Celebrities

America's top musicians, athletes, actors, and other celebrities are on the devil's agenda widely publicized by the country. Hence why you hear Jay-Z say, "Jesus can't save you. Life starts when the church ends," in affirmation of how their full dominion will begin after Christ raptures the church. The rapper who raps the line proclaims his fans won't get raptured, so be careful who you idolize and how you rap or sing along to their Luciferian songs of indoctrination to hell. America's favorite athletes are those who never mention the name of Christ in terms of worship. This includes the current most famous athlete in the country, whom I once glorified for being exemplary, albeit before my awakening. America's forty-fourth cosigns people like an Israeli writer who openly challenges God Almighty, and that's someone millions of Black people look up to. Once again, the American government says, "In God we trust," but that god is Lucifer. They've teamed up with Lucifer's angels (sky gods) who guide them toward releasing their master from the abyss. That forty-eighth president will shock the world when his time comes, and I pray you're one of Christ's electors by 2030.

Every other religion calls the names of the specific gods they worship, and only the name of the Christian God was hidden. So when you hear other religions call the names of their gods, it is not Yahuah, so please note we do not worship the same god! Also, note that the name of the Christian God is "not Yahweh," as that is a name of yet another lesser god that was syncretized into Judaism to cause confusion and to lead many into worshiping a lesser deity. When you see the temple of a One World Religion that combines Islam, Judaism, and Catholicism (pagan Christianity) erected between

2026 and 2029, you'll know that Yahuah has truly sent me to convey this message.

There's proof of everything mentioned in the Holy Bible, down to archaeological findings of inscriptions that reference the Israelites and their God, Yahuah. Ancient kings of Egypt, Babylon, Assyria, Persia, Greece, and Rome all reference their experiences with the Israelites, Jews, and Yahuah, as depicted in scriptures. There are over 330,000 cross-references in the Holy Bible, identifying similar forewarnings, signs, and prophecies that continually manifest to this day and will continue to be fulfilled until the end of time. The Bible comprises compositions written by forty men, most of whom never met each other. The scriptures were written in three different languages, on three different continents over thousands of years, and such synchronicity is impossible to accomplish if these humans weren't influenced by Yahuah.

Lesser gods have led men to write what presents to be kindergarten context filled with one man's claims, with nothing to juxtapose against or cross-reference for validity. The Bible isn't written by ordinary men, but by prophets that operated under the divine guidance of the Holy Spirit. Some of these prophets were literally fed scrolls by Yahusha, which they ate and then regurgitated in words, rewritten by the hands of man. Christ in spirit fed Isaiah, John, and Ezekiel. Christ in flesh taught several apostles. Christ alone fulfilled over three hundred prophecies from His birth in flesh to His ascension to glory. Any book, mantra, epistle, or mythological composition pales in comparison; as such, there is no comparison. As seen in 2 Timothy 3:16, "All scripture is God-breathed," so please stop saying "men wrote the Bible" because no conglomerate of men is capable of such divine abilities. The Bible is the living word of our living God revealed through chosen men who were found worthy of witnessing the omniscience, omnipresence, and omnipotence of Yahuah, God Almighty.

That said, do not play with the name of Yahuah, for whoever does so may be condemned to eternal suffering. Please govern yourself with proper decorum when conducting research to verify every claim I've presented, and be wary of false prophets because we live in a world where everyone with a microphone and camera believes they know what they know not about. Pray for spiritual discernment before you dive into the facts so that you're not led astray, and once you find these things to be true, strengthen your faith and only seek advice from trusted sources. I'm a warrior for Yahuah and His one true messiah, Yahusha, also known as Jesus Christ. I prefer to call Him by His true name, but that doesn't invalidate your preference.

Our world is at the boiling point of Yahuah's judgment, and the signs foretold of thousands of years ago are unfolding before our eyes. You see the Euphrates River drying up, the Jordan River drying up, hundreds of thousands of fish washed ashore, clouds have fallen from the skies, the earthquakes have begun. The unification of worlds through the English language and their coordinated activities to unleash Lucifer through CERN's hadron collider is reminiscent of the Tower of Babel. Sodom and Gomorrah pale in comparison to the sexual immorality peddled across the world by the United States. It's said in Revelation 9 that Abaddon (Lucifer) was given the key to the abyss. Abaddon is the Hebrew name of the god known as the destroyer, who is known to the Greeks as Apollyon and to the Hindus as Shiva. Remember I mentioned these gods are all the same, bearing different names in different regions. Shiva's statue is erected at the campus of CERN, whose opening ceremony was a ritual to Satan, and they continually display subcurrents of demon worship at their events. All these signs are before us, and some end-time woes listed in the book of Revelation have been unfolding before our very eyes.

I need you to know and understand that the Scriptures of Yahuah are the only true written words that stand the test of time. Comparing books of other religions to The Holy Bible is like bringing a camel to compete at the Miss Universe Pageant. They have no business being in the same space or category. The Holy Bible stands alone, light-years apart from everything in existence—they contain the unquestionable truth of life in entirety and encompass what was, what is, and is to come. Several additional books that complete the puzzle were banned by the Roman Catholic Church, but what we have in the Holy Bible is plenty enough. You'll notice I kept everything in this letter within the confines of the sixty-six books given unto us through the institution that politicized religion and soured it's taste in the mouth of people around the world, thus leading to hundreds of denominations.

Remain strong, for amidst the chaos lies a pocket of solitude for those who keep their eyes on Christ. Peter walked on water when his eyes remained on Christ, and he didn't sink until he got distracted by the winds. The vices of the Western worlds are winds of distraction that drown us in sin. Everything has been curated, tailored, and directed to keep our minds on sexual immorality, perversion, lust, ignorance, violence, addiction, and gluttony. It's impossible to turn on the radio without hearing male and female artists spew lust and violent gibberish. TV shows are laced with perversion, down to cartoons, which are now used to force gender confusion and suggestive sodomy onto kids.

Transgenders are allowed to nurture little babies at schools, and adult men showcase themselves as drag queens to innocent babies. They force-feed it through all media outlets and have made their way onto the pulpits of many churches. You must pray for spiritual discernment even before you fully immerse yourself with a church, for there are many false prophets leading the world astray every single Sunday. I speak to you with God's wisdom as no other man could teach me any of the things I know, of which what I share in this letter is only a fragment. I haven't been intimidated to say anything beyond some surface-level things addressed in this letter.

> Where is the wise person? Where is the teacher of the law? Where is the philosopher of this age? Has not God made foolish the wisdom of the world? For since in the wisdom of God the world through its wisdom did not know him, God was pleased through the foolishness of what was preached to save those who believe. Jews demand signs and Greeks look for wisdom, but we preach Christ crucified: a stumbling block to Jews and foolishness to Gentiles, but to those whom God has called, both Jews and Greeks, Christ the

AMERICA'S 48TH PRESIDENT AND THE MORNING STAR—THE TWO KINGS OF TYRE

power of God and the wisdom of God. For the foolishness of God is wiser than human wisdom, and the weakness of God is stronger than human strength". (1 Corinthians 1:20–25)

You need the Holy Spirit to understand these things in its entirety. We cannot rely on our knowledge for it was given unto us by man and is flawed from inception.

Yahuah's Wisdom Revealed by the Spirit

We do, however, speak a message of wisdom among the mature, but not the wisdom of this age or of the rulers of this age, who are coming to nothing. No, we declare God's wisdom, a mystery that has been hidden and that God destined for our glory before time began. None of the rulers of this age understood it, for if they had, they would not have crucified the Lord of glory. However, as it is written: "What no eye has seen, what no ear has heard, and what no human mind has conceived"— the things God has prepared for those who love him—these are the things God has revealed to us by his Spirit. The Spirit searches all things, even the deep things of God. For who knows a person's thoughts except their own spirit within them? In the same way no one knows the thoughts of God except the Spirit of God. What we have received is not the spirit of the world, but the Spirit who is from God, so that we may understand what God has freely given us. This is what we speak, not in words taught us by human wisdom but in words taught by the Spirit, explaining spiritual realities with Spirit-taught words. The person without the Spirit does not accept the things that come from the Spirit of

AMERICA'S 48ᵀᴴ PRESIDENT AND THE MORNING STAR—THE TWO KINGS OF TYRE

God but considers them foolishness, and cannot understand them because they are discerned only through the Spirit. (1 Corinthians 2:6–14)

All it takes to receive the Holy Spirit is to surrender yourself to our Creator, to seek Him earnestly, and to pray for grace. I've been on this journey for only six months and within that timeframe, I've been blessed with wisdom and knowledge that eluded me for over three decades of my existence. Even the wisest man King Solomon, reckoned with accepting the fear of God as the beginning of wisdom, and to know Him is understanding. Proverbs 9:11–12 says, "For through wisdom your days will be many, and years will be added to your life. If you are wise, your wisdom will reward you..." James 1:5 also says, "If any of you lacks wisdom, you should ask God, who gives generously to all without finding fault, and it will be given to you." You cannot gain wisdom from God without asking Him.

When tempted, no one should say, "God is tempting me." For God cannot be tempted by evil, nor does he tempt anyone; but each person is tempted when they are dragged away by their own evil desire and enticed. Then, after desire has conceived, it gives birth to sin; and sin, when it is full-grown, gives birth to death." (James 1:13–15)

Those verses assert you can't blame God for anything. The flesh is sold to sin by way of the disobedience of our ancestors passed down to us. God in His infinite mercy sacrificed His only True Son to die for our sins, paying the price to reverse the curse and redeem us from eternal death. We must remain thankful not only for the Son but also for the Father who sent His Son to guide us, first as a God and then in the flesh. We must also revere the Holy Spirit who dwells amongst us until the allotted time is up. The Father, the Son, and the Holy Spirit are inseparable, for they are God in one and all in God, indivisibly working in one accord to save us from this wicked world. I pray you relent from ascribing any blame unto God and ask forgiveness for questioning Him in any capacity. We're nothing but clay in the hands of the potter, and although we could be discarded of quite easily, He tempers His judgment, giving us every chance to realize our misdeeds, and thus return to His favor.

It's important to know that all the lesser gods worshipped by these nations always lead them to ruins. Also more important to note is that Yahuah showed His superiority above them all, through the *true* Israelites. Ancient Egyptian gods were all disgraced and powerless when Yahusha used Moses to strike them with ten plagues. The Persian gods were powerless before Yahusha, King Nebuchadnezzar II of Babylon was turned into a beast for seven years, after which he proclaimed Yahuah as the true God of all gods, and so forth. Egypt, Assyria, Babylon, Greece, and Rome were once mighty nations that now lay in ruins, with nothing but old dusty statues to commemorate their existence. Yet modern nations like America model everything they do after them, erect the same monuments to those gods, and follow suit in their methods of supremacy and dominance by warfare. Its apparent the fate that will eventually befall America unless the nation repents like Nineveh did when Jonah took the word of Yahuah to them. Corrupt nations like this are known for persecuting true messengers of Yahuah, which is why Jonah tried to elude the mission. Come what may though, I'm ready to sing the tune of our Father in heaven until the day I take my last breath in this condemned flesh we inhabit.

Anyways, several curses have been reversed over the course of time as God's anger doesn't endure forever. The *Curse of Babel* was reversed at Pentecost when the Holy Spirit came upon the apostles, and they spoke in tongues, meaning people from different nations could understand their own languages as they spoke. The language barrier was broken, thus allowing them to minister to people from all walks of life. The *Curse of Flesh* was broken at Crucifixion, by Christ who died for our sins and offered us salvation in exchange for believing in Him. Once you proclaim Christ as your savior and get baptized, you become born in spirit and shed all the condemnation the flesh comes with. The *Curse of Ignorance* is being broken and many are waking up to seek Yahusha, to know Him, and to understand His Kingdom is at hand.

No One Is Righteous

What shall we conclude then? Do we have any advantage? Not at all! For we have already made the charge that Jews and Gentiles alike are all under the power of sin. As it is written: "There is no one righteous, not even one; there is no one who understands; there is no one who seeks God. All have turned away, they have together become worthless; there is no one who does good, not even one." "Their throats are open graves; their tongues practice deceit." "The poison of vipers is on their lips." "Their mouths are full of cursing and bitterness." "Their feet are swift to shed blood; ruin and misery mark their ways, and the way of peace they do not know." "There is no fear of God before their eyes." (Hebrews 3:9–18)

Verse 9 expresses that everyone is sold to sin. There's not a single righteous being on earth because the flesh is flawed. Righteousness is perfection and only Christ was perfect. The rest of us are sinful. Verses 10–18 go on to confirm it's written (in Scriptures) that mankind doesn't understand and seek God. It goes on to list the sins and wickedness of mankind, concluding that the fear of God eludes man, for we'd refrain from most sinful things if we truly fear God.

> Now we know that whatever the law says, it says to those who are under the law, so that every

AMERICA'S 48TH PRESIDENT AND THE MORNING STAR—THE TWO KINGS OF TYRE

mouth may be silenced and the whole world held accountable to God. Therefore no one will be declared righteous in God's sight by the works of the law; rather, through the law we become conscious of our sin. (Hebrews 3:19–20)

The "law" means scriptures, and in this case, it means "commandments." By this, all mankind shall be judged, as that's the measuring stick by which we're held accountable. It goes on to say no one will be declared righteous in God's sight if they're being held accountable strictly by how they adhere to the commandments. The commandments are basically to make us aware of our sins.

Righteousness Through Faith

But now apart from the law the righteousness of God has been made known, to which the Law and the Prophets testify. This righteousness is given through faith in Jesus Christ to all who believe. There is no difference between Jew and Gentile, for all have sinned and fall short of the glory of God, and all are justified freely by his grace through the redemption that came by Christ Jesus. God presented Christ as a sacrifice of atonement, through the shedding of his blood—to be received by faith. He did this to demonstrate his righteousness, because in his forbearance he had left the sins committed beforehand unpunished—he did it to demonstrate his righteousness at the present time, so as to be just and the one who justifies those who have faith in Jesus." (Hebrews 3:21–26)

You don't have to be "righteous" to be saved. Remember righteousness is impossible to achieve in this flesh that's condemned to sin. Now righteousness is through faith in Christ. He achieved righteousness and took our sins away through His sacrifice. Christ bridged the gap between Jews and Gentiles, so now salvation isn't limited to His people but to all who believe in Him. Christ continually atones our sins in perpetuity *if* we remain steadfast in our faith in Him. Here's confirmation in another scripture:

AMERICA'S 48TH PRESIDENT AND THE MORNING STAR—THE TWO KINGS OF TYRE

During the days of Jesus' life on earth, he offered up prayers and petitions with fervent cries and tears to the one who could save him from death, and he was heard because of his reverent submission. Son though he was, he learned obedience from what he suffered and, once made perfect, he became the source of eternal salvation for all who obey him. (Hebrews 5:7–10)

Day after day every priest stands and performs his religious duties; again and again he offers the same sacrifices, which can never take away sins. But when this priest had offered for all time one sacrifice for sins, he sat down at the right hand of God, and since that time he waits for his enemies to be made his footstool. For by one sacrifice he has made perfect forever those who are being made holy". (Hebrews 10:11–14)

Hebrews 10 confirms what I said earlier that sacrifices of lambs didn't take away sins because they had to be done repeatedly. However, this Priest (Christ) saved us with His one sacrifice that lasts for all time.

The body, however, is not meant for sexual immorality but for the Lord, and the Lord for the body. By his power God raised the Lord from the dead, and he will raise us also. Do you not know that your bodies are members of Christ himself? Shall I then take the members of Christ and unite them with a prostitute? Never! Do you not know that he who unites himself with a prostitute is one with her in body? For it is said, "The two will become one flesh." But whoever is united with the Lord is one with him in spirit.

Christ said, "The knowledge of the secrets of the kingdom of God has been given to you, but to others I speak in parables, so that, 'though seeing, they may not see; though hearing, they may not understand.'" Many indeed see but are blind, they hear, but they do not understand. Christ once came in the flesh to teach, and He's coming back to judge, but people like me are being raised to help the blind see, and to minister understanding unto minds that have been dulled by this wicked world. I speak not of my own volition but of the Holy Spirit, one with the Father and Son, operating in synchrony to pass along the message of redemption and paradise.

Yahuah, God almighty, is who we are mostly eternally thankful for, because everything Christ did was for our sake, through Him who chose Christ and sent Him to do what needed to be done. He gave Christ the strength, the glory, and the power to conquer evil. Without Him, Christ would've stayed dead, but Yahuah raised Him, bringing the sacrificed lamb back to life, so His blood can live forever to save us in perpetuity until Judgment Day when sin is completely removed from the world, and we inherit our new bodies that are immune to sin.

Please I beg you, stop allowing your innocent babies to listen to worldly music about sex, drugs, and violence. It seems harmless and cute, but that's how they slowly normalized sexual immorality to the point where marriages and stable homes have become completely obscure. I once was a part of those who reveled in secular music, but my soul has since been apprehended for a greater cause, and I refuse to peddle that which leads people astray. Being godly doesn't eliminate joy and you'll be surprised to realize there's no greater joy than that gifted by the Holy Spirit.

I've emphatically passed the warning along to the nation of America, now I must also pass along a message to the People of Yehuda, black people.

> Jerusalem, Jerusalem, you who kill the prophets
> and stone those sent to you, how often I have
> longed to gather your children together, as a hen
> gathers her chicks under her wings, and you were

not willing. Look, your house is left to you desolate. For I tell you, you will not see me again until you say, "Blessed is he who comes in the name of the Yahuah."

Christ emphatically expressed His reproach for Jerusalem because of their refusal to accept Him. He curses the geographical land of Jerusalem and proclaims that His people won't see Him again until they are all "blessed is He who comes in the name of Yahuah." That phrase presents an expression of what The people of Yehuda must do to get back in His graces. The significance of Christ saying this is that He wants us to receive Him wholeheartedly, love Him, celebrate Him, praise Him, and appreciate Him. That's all He asks—a warm reception and proclamation of His glory without hesitation. I'll help you understand why Christ said this.

> They brought [the donkey] to Yeshuah, threw their cloaks on the colt and put Yeshuah on it. As he went along, people spread their cloaks on the road. When he came near the place where the road goes down the Mount of Olives, the whole crowd of disciples began joyfully to praise God in loud voices for all the miracles they had seen: "Blessed is the king who comes in the name of the Lord!" "Peace in heaven and glory in the highest!" (Luke 19:35–37)

It's evident such reception and proclamation is what Yeshuah expects from His people, so please gather as people, fellowship with your brethren, and proclaim the glory of our Messiah, chanting, "Blessed is Yeshuah who comes in the name of Yahuah!" Proclaim it in your heart, feel it in your soul, and watch the glory of our Messiah move mountains in your life. You will be rescued by the mighty arm of the Anointed One who will return with His iron scepter to smash these wicked nations like pottery.

Israel's Call to Glory

> The Lord was very angry with your ancestors. Therefore tell the people: This is what Yahuah Almighty says: 'Return to me,' declares Yahuah Almighty, 'and I will return to you,' says Yahuah Almighty. Do not be like your ancestors, to whom the earlier prophets proclaimed: This is what the Lord Almighty says: 'Turn from your evil ways and your evil practices.' But they would not listen or pay attention to me, declares Yahuah. Where are your ancestors now? And the prophets, do they live forever? But did not my words and my decrees, which I commanded my servants the prophets, overtake your ancestors?
> —Zechariah 1:2–6

This is a reiteration of Matthew 23 where Christ says He's departing from us until we give Him the praise He deserves. Once again, proclaim it to the heavens and make it a part of your daily routine to glorify the name of He who comes in the name of our Father.

> "When I called, they did not listen; so when they called, I would not listen," says Yahuah Almighty. "I scattered them with a whirlwind among all the nations, where they were strangers. The land they left behind them was so desolate that no one traveled through it. This is how they made the pleasant land desolate." (Zechariah 7:13–14)

AMERICA'S 48ᵀᴴ PRESIDENT AND THE MORNING STAR—THE TWO KINGS OF TYRE

This is what Yahuah Almighty says: "I will save my people from the countries of the east and the west. I will bring them back to live in Jerusalem; they will be my people, and I will be faithful and righteous to them as their God, "This is what Yahuah Almighty says: "In those days ten people from all languages and nations will take firm hold of one Jew by the hem of his robe and say, 'Let us go with you, because we have heard that God is with you.'"(Zechariah 8:7–8, 23)

I referenced Zechariah 7 to emphasize truly and certainly that black people were indeed the Jews that were scattered across nations. Zechariah 8 then reaffirms that the grace of Yahuah will return to the true Jews (black people) and that in the end times, people will cling unto them for the hand of Yahuah will be upon them.

"Come, Zion! Escape, you who live in Daughter Babylon!" For this is what Yahuah Almighty says: "After the Glorious One has sent me against the nations that have plundered you—for whoever touches you touches the apple of his eye—I will surely raise my hand against them so that their slaves will plunder them.[b] Then you will know that the Lord Almighty has sent me. "Shout and be glad, Daughter Zion. For I am coming, and I will live among you," declares the Lord. "Many nations will be joined with Yahuah in that day and will become my people. I will live among you and you will know that Yahuah Almighty has sent me to you. Yahuah will inherit Judah as his portion in the holy land and will again choose Jerusalem. Be still before Yahuah, all mankind, because he has roused himself from his holy dwelling." (Zechariah 2:7–13)

It's evident from these scriptures once again that Yahuah allowed the people of Yehuda (black people, the true Jews) to be held in captivity by nations described as Babylon. According to the scriptures, Babylon is used to depict Ancient Babylon, and Babylon is also used to depict modern-day United States and United Kingdom. The Jews were once held captive in Ancient Babylon, and the Jews were once again held captive in modern-day Babylon (America and Britain). Now Christ says He's coming to live amongst His people during His millennial reign on earth, after the upcoming tribulation. Christ makes it known that these nations called Babylon will plunder the slaves.

Notice how Ancient Babylon isn't prophesied to become plundered in return by the slaves, but that modern Babylon will become plundered by the slaves because the modern era is when He returns. Meaning when Christ returns, black people will become masters to the people who enslaved them. Please note that although Jews are a part of Israel, not all Israelites are Jews. The tribe of Yehuda is a separate group of people from the southern Kingdom of Israel. They are predominantly black-skinned, which is why Christ was prophesied to be dark-skinned in the Holy Book.

> *Blow the trumpet in Zion; sound the alarm on my holy hill. Let all who live in the land tremble, for the day of Yeshuah is coming. It is close at hand—a day of darkness and gloom, a day of clouds and blackness."* "Even now," declares Yeshuah, "return to me with all your heart, with fasting and weeping and mourning." Rend your heart and not your garments. Return to Yeshuah your God, for he is gracious and compassionate, slow to anger and abounding in love, and he relents from sending calamity. Who knows? He may turn and relent and leave behind a blessing— grain offerings and drink offerings for the Lord your God". (Joel 2:1–2 and 12–14)

AMERICA'S 48TH PRESIDENT AND THE MORNING STAR—THE TWO KINGS OF TYRE

Once again, the referenced book of Joel is an end-time prophecy for this generation, regarding the kingdom of Christ to come in less than a decade from now. The second portion showcases what must be done to avert calamity or at least to remain blessed amidst all the chaos to ensue.

> Nevertheless, I have this against you: You tolerate that woman Jezebel, who calls herself a prophet. By her teaching she misleads my servants into sexual immorality and the eating of food sacrificed to idols. I have given her time to repent of her immorality, but she is unwilling. So I will cast her on a bed of suffering, and I will make those who commit adultery with her suffer intensely, unless they repent of her ways. I will strike her children dead. Then all the churches will know that I am he who searches hearts and minds, and I will repay each of you according to your deeds". (Revelation 2:14 and 20–23)

This shows how modern-day Israelites and Jews (black people) are unknowingly tricked by Jezebel (Roman Catholic Church) into eating food sacrificed to idols. This refers to pagan feasts and holidays like Valentine's Day (Lupercalia, for sexual immorality), Christmas Day (dedicated to pagan gods), Easter (dedicated to goddess Ishtar), Halloween, and so forth. Black people unknowingly engage in these things that Yahuah detests. Most of these "holidays" were sanctioned by the Roman Catholic Church who are devil worshippers claiming to be followers of Christ. I mentioned this before, but I had to say it louder for the people in the back!

This brings me to the final scriptures I'll quote in full confirmation of how those known to be Israelites today are *not* the true Israelites. I put the modern-day names of the referenced locations in parentheses, so you know where the prophesied destructions are taking place.

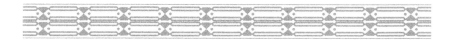

Judgment on Israel's Enemies

A prophecy: The word of the Lord is against the land of Hadrak (INDIA) IN and will come to rest on Damascus— (SYRIA) SY for the eyes of all people and all the tribes of Israel are on the Lord— and on Hamath too, which borders on it, and on Tyre and Sidon (ISREAL IL and LEBANON LB), though they are very skillful. Tyre has built herself a stronghold; she has heaped up silver like dust, and gold like the dirt of the streets. But Yahuah will take away her possessions and destroy her power on the sea, and she will be consumed by fire. Ashkelon will see it and fear; (ISRAEL IL) Gaza will writhe in agony, (PALESTINE PS) and Ekron (CENTRAL ISRAEL IL) too, for her hope will wither. Gaza (PALESTINE PS) will lose her king and Ashkelon (ISRAEL IL) will be deserted. A mongrel people will occupy Ashdod (ISRAEL IL) and I will put an end to the pride of the Philistines (GREEKS GR) I will take the blood from their mouths, the forbidden food from between their teeth. Those who are left will belong to our God and become a clan in Judah, and Ekron (ISRAEL IL) will be like the Jebusites (original Canaanites that were displaced by Israelites). But I will encamp at my temple to guard it against marauding forces. Never

AMERICA'S 48TH PRESIDENT AND THE MORNING STAR—THE TWO KINGS OF TYRE

again will an oppressor overrun my people, for now I am keeping watch." (Zechariah 9:1–8)

Current inhabitants of the geographical space called Israel are not the true Israelites but are enemies of the true people of Israel. The geographical location of Israel will be entrenched in wars from now until April 7, 2027, after which an abominable One World Religion temple will be built on the site of Yahuah's former Temple. The purpose of this message isn't to spew hate toward the imposters but to help you understand what's to come for black people when they do what Christ expects, which is to praise Him, seek Him, and proclaim His name.

This brings me to the last scripture I'll quote, directed specifically at The United States of America and her coven of evil-headed eagles. The country for whom this letter is intended. The country in collusion with the False Israelites and the fake Jews. The nation that's secretly spearheading efforts to unleash Lucifer from the abyss. The country who will become successful in doing so by the forty-eighth president. The country foolishly thinking they can manufacture enough weapons to blast asteroids sent unto earth from the heavens. The country that truly believes it can coordinate an army through its European allies to fight Christ and His angels at the Battle of Armageddon when our savior returns. America, this is for you!

A Prophecy Against the King of Tyre

The word of Yahusha came to me: "Son of man, say to the ruler of Tyre, 'This is what the Sovereign Lord says: "'In the pride of your heart you say, "I am a god; I sit on the throne of a god in the heart of the seas." But you are a mere mortal and not a god, though you think you are as wise as a god. Are you wiser than Daniel? Is no secret hidden from you? By your wisdom and understanding you have gained wealth for yourself and amassed gold and silver in your treasuries. By your great skill in trading, you have increased your wealth, and because of your wealth your heart has grown proud."' Therefore this is what the Sovereign Lord says: "'Because you think you are wise, as wise as a god, I am going to bring foreigners against you, the most ruthless of nations; they will draw their swords against your beauty and wisdom and pierce your shining splendor. They will bring you down to the pit, and you will die a violent death in the heart of the seas. Will you then say, 'I am a god,' in the presence of those who kill you? You will be but a mortal, not a god, in the hands of those who slay you. You will die the death of the uncircumcised at the hands of foreigners. I have spoken, declares the Sovereign Lord.'" (Ezekiel 28:1–10)

AMERICA'S 48TH PRESIDENT AND THE MORNING STAR—THE TWO KINGS OF TYRE

Analysis

Please understand that I'm operating with Yahuah's perfect wisdom and everything you're about to read in this analysis is not of my reasoning but of God's true wisdom. This first portion of the prophecy is directed at a mortal ruler who sits on the throne of a lesser god—known as the devil, Lucifer, or the dragon. The book of Ezekiel was written around 590 BC, so although the chapter I quoted was prophesied around two thousand six hundred and fourteen (2,614) years ago, the referenced ruler is yet to come, even as of this day in year AD 2024. This ruler is going to be the 48 president of the United States as I mentioned earlier in "Prophecy 5" of this letter. Verse 3 makes a remark about Prophet Daniel solely because The book of Daniel also prophesies of this End Time ruler, as seen in Daniel chapter 11 and 12 below:

The King Who Exalts Himself

> The king will do as he pleases. He will exalt and magnify himself above every god and will say unheard-of things against the God of gods. He will be successful until the time of wrath is completed. He will attack the mightiest fortresses with the help of a foreign god and will greatly honor those who acknowledge him. He will make them rulers over many people and will distribute the land at a price. He will pitch his royal tents between the seas at the beautiful holy mountain. Yet he will come to his end, and no one will help him. (Daniel 11:36, 39, and 45)

> At that time Michael, the great prince who protects your people, will arise. There will be a time of distress such as has not happened from the beginning of nations until then. But at that time your people—everyone whose name is found written

127

in the book—will be delivered. Multitudes who sleep in the dust of the earth will awake: some to everlasting life, others to shame and everlasting contempt. Those who are wise will shine like the brightness of the heavens, and those who lead many to righteousness, like the stars for ever and ever. But you, Daniel, roll up and seal the words of the scroll until the time of the end. (Daniel 12:1–4)

I quoted those scriptures to help any reader fully understand why Daniel was mentioned in Ezekiel 28:3. Daniel operated on Yahuah's wisdom and wrote based on the visions given unto him and through the influence of the Holy Spirit. You'll see the verses I quoted from the book of Daniel specifically focus on the end times. People around the world have struggled to decipher Daniel's prophecies and have only been able to understand fulfilled portions, whilst they claim the other parts to be incorrect. There's nothing incorrect about Daniel's prophesies, and they can only be understood through higher levels of God's wisdom, that which I can humbly assert to have been given. From this point, I'll return to the "king of Tyre" in Ezekiel 28:1–10.

Verses 4–5 of Ezekiel 28 are metaphorically referring to how The United States (the throne this ruler sits upon) has amassed an insurmountable amount of power and wealth through earthly wisdom, thus leading to his pride. The rest of the verses go on to condemn the ruler, with verse 10 saying, "*You will die the death of the uncircumcised at the hands of foreigners*," which is an ancient figure of speech that's utilized in this context to describe the fate of Europeans at the hands of God's true chosen people, you know, the ones who truly have the culture of circumcision on the eighth day, as seen in the Old Testament, the ones uncircumcised slavers have held captive in different episodes of life from Ancient Babylon before Christ until modern-day slavery was abolished just a few hundred years ago.

There are other scriptures that go into more detail, where God says "I will bend Judah as I bend my bow and fill it with Ephraim. I

AMERICA'S 48TH PRESIDENT AND THE MORNING STAR—THE TWO KINGS OF TYRE

will rouse your sons, Zion, against your sons, Greece…" That means the true descendants of Yehuda (Jews) and the true descendants of Ephraim (Israel) will conquer the descendants of the Greeks. I mentioned earlier that Greece was conquered by the Romans, then a portion of Rome was conquered by the Islamic Ottomans. These are the peoples that enslaved the true descendants of Israel, and the true Jews, holding them in captivity until they later formed European nations and joined forces to recapture the true people of Yehuda (true Jews) that had migrated away from their lands.

Through Ezekiel 28:1–10, I've helped you understand the King of Tyre is the end-time ruler of America, specifically the forty-eighth president scheduled to assume office in 2028. I used pertinent verses from the Book of Daniel chapters 11 and 12 to collate the revelations given to me on this matter. We've seen Ezekiel 28:1–10, so let's proceed to the other half that culminates the fate to befall America and the beast she serves.

> The word of the Lord came to me: "Son of man, take up lament concerning the king of Tyre and say to him: 'This is what the Sovereign Lord says: "'You were the seal of perfection, full of wisdom and perfect in beauty. You were in Eden, the garden of God; every precious stone adorned you: carnelian, chrysolite and emerald, topaz, onyx and jasper, lapis lazuli, turquoise and beryl. Your settings and mountings were made of gold; on the day you were created they were prepared. You were anointed as a guardian cherub, for so I ordained you. You were on the holy mount of God; you walked among the fiery stones. You were blameless in your ways from the day you were created till wickedness was found in you. Through your widespread trade you were filled with violence, and you sinned. So I drove you in disgrace from the mount of God, and I expelled you, guardian cherub, from among the fiery

stones. Your heart became proud on account of your beauty, and you corrupted your wisdom because of your splendor. So I threw you to the earth; I made a spectacle of you before kings. By your many sins and dishonest trade you have desecrated your sanctuaries. So I made a fire come out from you, and it consumed you, and I reduced you to ashes on the ground in the sight of all who were watching. All the nations who knew you are appalled at you; you have come to a horrible end and will be no more."' (Ezekiel 28:12–19)

This King of Tyre in the second portion of Ezekiel 28 represents Lucifer, who is the god worshipped by the mortal king of Tyre mentioned in the first ten verses. To clarify, the first King of Tyre is a mortal ruler, while this other King of Tyre is the god served by that mortal ruler. I've mentioned throughout this letter that America's god is not the Christian God as they portray it to be. Rather, they worship an array of sky gods, all of whom are under the supremacy of their main lord, Lucifer.

Lucifer's name translates to Morning Star and confirmation is seen in Isaiah 12, which says, "How you have fallen from heaven, morning star, son of the dawn." The fall of Lucifer referenced in Isaiah 12 is documented in Revelation 12 which I'll quote below.

Then another sign appeared in heaven: an enormous red dragon with seven heads and ten horns and seven crowns on its heads. Its tail swept a third of the stars out of the sky and flung them to the earth. "Then war broke out in heaven. Michael and his angels fought against the dragon, and the dragon and his angels fought back. But he was not strong enough, and they lost their place in heaven. The great dragon was hurled down— that ancient serpent called the devil, or Satan,

AMERICA'S 48TH PRESIDENT AND THE MORNING STAR—THE TWO KINGS OF TYRE

> who leads the whole world astray. He was hurled to the earth, and his angels with him. (Revelation 12:3–4 and 7–9)

The book of Revelation 12 gives an account of Lucifer's rebellion and how his corruption caused a third of the stars (a.k.a. evil angels, lesser gods, or sky gods) to fall from heaven. The verbiage metaphorically uses the dragon's tail to depict how the other stars lost their place in heaven, for wherever the body goes, the tail follows. Hence, Lucifer is the body of corruption and the angels he recruited lost their place for following him like a tail. This goes to prove that all the sky gods, disembodied Nephilim, celestial beings, fallen angels, and evil entities I've mentioned throughout this letter, operate under one main commander who through all these entities influence worldly rulers to lead the world astray. Now in the book of Revelation 9, when the end-time trumpets are going off in the heavens to effect final judgments on earth, Lucifer is finally unleashed from the Abyss.

> The fifth angel sounded his trumpet, and I saw a star that had fallen from the sky to the earth. The star was given the key to the shaft of the Abyss. When he opened the Abyss, smoke rose from it like the smoke from a gigantic furnace. The sun and sky were darkened by the smoke from the Abyss. And out of the smoke locusts came down on the earth and were given power like that of scorpions of the earth. They had tails with stingers, like scorpions, and in their tails they had power to torment people for five months. They had as king over them the angel of the Abyss, whose name in Hebrew is Abaddon and in Greek is Apollyon (that is, Destroyer). (Revelation 9:1–3 and 10–11)

Here I am in shock as to how the Holy Spirit has methodically brought things full circle once again in this letter. Revelation 9 ties into 'Prophecy '5 I gave earlier on, and it piggybacks off Revelation 12. We saw Lucifer fall in Revelation 12, along with his fallen angels who account for a third (33 percent) of all the angels in heaven at the time of his fall. Although Lucifer was allowed to reign on the earth, he was bound at some point, which is narrated in Revelation 20 below.

> "And I saw an angel coming down out of heaven, having the key to the Abyss and holding in his hand a great chain. He seized the dragon, that ancient serpent, who is the devil, or Satan, and bound him for a thousand years. He threw him into the Abyss, and locked and sealed it over him, to keep him from deceiving the nations anymore until the thousand years were ended. After that, he must be set free for a short time. When the thousand years are over, Satan will be released from his prison and will go out to deceive the nations in the four corners of the earth—Gog and Magog— and to gather them for battle. In number they are like the sand on the seashore. They marched across the breadth of the earth and surrounded the camp of God's people, the city he loves. But fire came down from heaven and devoured them". (Revelation 20:1–3 and 7–9)

Stick with me on how these ties back into the book of Ezekiel chapter 28 regarding the mortal ruler introduced as king of Tyre, the god referenced as King of Tyre, and how they're both relevant to the United States of America and the end-time judgment that's knocking on her bald head. I already expressed that the mortal king of Tyre described in verses 1–10 of Ezekiel 28 alludes to the forty-eight president of the United States who will assume office in 2028. I've also expressed that the god denoted as King of Tyre is Lucifer, who once was a glorious angel in the heavens as described in Ezekiel 28, cast onto earth in Revelation 12, locked in the abyss in Revelation 20, and finally given the keys to the abyss by his loyal servants in Revelation 9.

I proclaimed earlier in this letter that America is secretly behind the operation to unleash Abaddon through the Hadron Collider operated by CERN. Abaddon is known as Apollyon the destroyer to the Greeks, and as Shiva the god of destruction to the Hindus. This is why the statue of Shiva was 'gifted' to the CERN by the Indian government, just as the Egyptian government 'gifted' a pair of Ancient Egyptian Obelisks (Cleopatra's needles) to the United Kingdom and the United States. The rulers of these nations worship Lucifer and his angels, and they're making harmonized efforts to raise their lord and master from the abyss. They will be successful by 2029 when America becomes the throne of the dragon (Lucifer) and the leader of his worldwide army. America's forty-eighth president will be the ruler of the dragon's kingdom. So once again, if I'm not here when it happens, let this letter serve as an affirmation that Yahuah, our God Almighty spoke through me, and whoever is privileged to read the contents of this letter can follow the guidelines provided to save their souls or remain under the protection of Christ our Savior. Now that I've painted the full picture of who and what the kings of Tyre stand for, allow me to explain the end of this chasmic quote I'm dissecting from the prophecy in chapter 28 of Prophet Ezekiel's book.

> By your many sins and dishonest trade you have desecrated your sanctuaries. So I made a fire come out from you, and it consumed you, and I reduced you to ashes on the ground in the sight of all who were watching. All the nations who knew you are appalled at you; you have come to a horrible end and will be no more. (Ezekiel 28:18–19)

Here we see a similar situation to Genesis 3:14 where Yahuah cursed the serpent for tricking Eve into sin. The 'serpent' was an animal with limbs, probably a beautiful creature that appeared very innocent, like a bunny, but Yahuah cursed it to become an ugly spectacle that crawls around. Same it is for Lucifer who once had an innocent name and perfect appearance of beauty, but got cursed into becoming an ugly dragon, with a consuming fire within its belly. The fate of Lucifer is seen in verse 19 where he gets defeated in the presence of all the nations that worship him.

Prior to gaining God's wisdom, the book of Revelation seemed like wild comics, and I understood nothing but simple-minded things. Now that I'm armed with God's wisdom, I understand everything and will dedicate my life to helping others understand how the word of God is indeed alive. The Holy Bible is woven into every fabric of our lives, times, and entire existence, documenting what was, what is, and what's to come. Now that you know what's coming, allow me to remind you of the quote from the book of Daniel 12, which says *"those who are wise will shine like the brightness of the heavens, and those who lead many to righteousness, like the stars forever and ever.*

I will shine like the brightness of the heavens, just like whoever joins this effort to spread this letter that can help lead souls to righteousness. In this letter, I've given the keys to redemption, what to avoid, what to observe, and how salvation is simply by testifying the name of Christ and accepting him as your savior. That's it! I wish you could see what I see, but please know the world as we know it is way more spiritual than it is physical, so I plead with you to wake up and enjoin yourself with the army of God almighty. Apostle Paul couldn't have said it any better:

The Armor of God

Finally, be strong in the Lord and in his mighty power. Put on the full armor of God, so that you can take your stand against the devil's schemes. For our struggle is not against flesh and blood, but against the rulers, against the authorities, against the powers of this dark world and against

AMERICA'S 48TH PRESIDENT AND THE MORNING STAR—THE TWO KINGS OF TYRE

the spiritual forces of evil in the heavenly realms. Therefore put on the full armor of God, so that when the day of evil comes, you may be able to stand your ground, and after you have done everything, to stand. Stand firm then, with the belt of truth buckled around your waist, with the breastplate of righteousness in place, and with your feet fitted with the readiness that comes from the gospel of peace. In addition to all this, take up the shield of faith, with which you can extinguish all the flaming arrows of the evil one. Take the helmet of salvation and the sword of the Spirit, which is the word of God. (Ephesians 6:10–17)

Only observe what you see in the Holy Bible, not what the pagan Roman Catholic Church tricked you into doing. I recently started observing Christ's supper at home with my family and it's a great feeling. We pray before reading Luke 22:16–20, John 6:53–58, and Matthew 26:26–30, and then we break bread and drink grape juice. This is one of the few things Christ asks us to do in remembrance of Him. Women of our generation put weeks of effort into dressing slutty for the Halloween parties of evil spirits but won't set ten minutes aside to observe Christ's simple ask. Please do better!

My message comes from a place of love and deep passion to help save souls from impending judgment. I'm completely unbiased and have been sure to condemn any and every false religion, including Christian establishments founded on blasphemous and adulterous doctrines. About 99.9 percent of these various Christian denominations don't fully align themselves with the true gospel of Christ, and anything that branched off Catholicism is definitely astray. These denominations deify humans as saints and lead people to observe festivals established in observance of lesser gods.

Other denominations like the Mormons are also founded on one man's claim of divine visions, hitched unto Christ. Please remove yourself from these wicked establishments so you don't partake in their punishment. Ignorance isn't an excuse, and an absence of knowledge doesn't help avert punishment, especially after you've been warned. Adam and Eve blamed each other and the serpent but all three of them got punished. Please I beg this nation to repent and do right, and I beg the citizens, young and old, rich and poor, black and white, to proclaim, BLESSED IS HE WHO COMES IN THE NAME OF YAHUAH!

If you're reading this, you're truly loved by He who created you, and that's why you're fitted you with a moral compass that'll lead you into His grace. You've placed much of your trust in humans who disappoint you time after time, so I implore you to give Christ a chance and see how your life transforms gloriously before your very eyes. I'm living proof of this, and I can testify to the divine phenomena that has taken over my soul and given my life new meaning that can never again be corrupted by, or enslaved to the forces of darkness. Trusting in Yahuah and walking in His obedience gifts eternal sustenance.

> You will surely forget your trouble, recalling it only as waters gone by. Life will be brighter than noonday, and darkness will become like morning. You will be secure, because there is hope; you will look about you and take your rest in safety. You will lie down, with no one to make you afraid, and many will court your favor. (Job 11:16–19)

I've shared a wealth of wisdom from God's perspective, but I'd be wrong to leave you without disseminating some wisdom from a human, just like you. So I'll surmise the end of the letter with an arrangement of a few wise words from myself, woven into a guide for which to govern your life in recognizance of all I discussed.

> "There's no love at first sight without physical attraction, which means you're willing to take a chance based on what you see. So, understand life is an illusion and you see better with your eyes closed, for the promise of faith is better than fool's gold. Pour good into those around you, but understand you'll never fill a basket with water.

AMERICA'S 48TH PRESIDENT AND THE MORNING STAR—THE TWO KINGS OF TYRE

Be wary of affiliations with unequally yoked minds – A swan can't be best friends with a hippopotamus, it'll lose its grace by getting dirty, all while destined to be crushed under playful guise. That's a plea to be content with those who accept your obsequious deference to what nurtures your soul, as opposed to what appeases their folly. A wise one doesn't contend with God's peace, but a fool seeks refuge in the devil's storm. I need you to understand the price of joy is what your heart feels, over that which your eyes see. Be beautiful how God created you and don't alter your appearance to fit anyone's standards, just like the peacock who said, "I'd rather look fly than fly." Men labor in vain unless their trust is in Christ, so matter how often a lizard raises its head, it'll never reach that of a giraffe. Go nourish your spirit with the essence of God and manifest your goals in his Glory. I pray this letter is a tether that won't sever but keep us together." (King Joel)

This word I've shared with you isn't something I'm regurgitating from another being, or taught by anyone, but that which is given to me directly from the Holy Spirit. I must now attend to my four-month-old little princess who has missed Daddy for the past eight days I've spent dividing her deserved attention to this letter. I pray you'll be blessed by this message and its contents in its entirety. Blessed are those who spread this gospel of truth, for any souls they help lead to righteousness through its contents shall be credited unto them in the heavens. May the love of Christ be upon you and may His light illuminate your path to His glory. HalleluYah!

Respectfully,
Joel OreOluwa Elijah LivingGod
King Joel.

About the Author

J oel LivingGod, America's forty-eighth president and the Morning Star.

Joel LivingGod is a successful businessman, philanthropist, and renowned music artist who performs under the moniker King Joel. He's the modern-day personification of 'a beautiful mind' that encapsulates the essence of logos by interweaving idioms from classical antiquity with an unconventional touch of modernity as his preferred form of articulation. As a man of many talents, he played college football, ran track, and competed in academic exposés before prioritizing his oratorical skills in poetry, songwriting, screenplays, and theatre, which led him to form a record label called Elision Records. A Georgia State University Alumni who previously personified a larger-than-life charisma and boisterous showmanship in the entertainment world, Joel has since turned his life around for a greater cause, which is simply to help save lives.